Living My Dreams

DARIA SILVANO BRUCE

ISBN
978-1-957378-57-2 (Paperback)
978-1-957378-56-5 (eBook)
978-1-957378-58-9 (Hardcover)

TABLE OF CONTENTS

DEDICATION

This book is dedicated to my family. My one and only son and to the love of his life, my daughter- in- law, my three sweet granddaughters; I love them all very much. They are amazing! They have shown me that, no matter what happens in life, must always smile and continue living in our ordinary way. Be thankful for everything what we have.

To my two brothers and four sisters and the love of their lives, to my nieces and nephews, and to the rest in the immediate family circle; I love you, all.

In memoriam, a special dedication goes out to my departed loved ones: my husband, my parents, and my sister who never gave up on a tremendous fire (she died at the age of sixty-two). I miss you, and I love you, all. May the Lord bless you and bring you, all to the everlasting life.

To all the ones I loved before, to all my friends, and all my relatives around the world. I love you, all.

I live loving you. Thank you for loving me, as well.

Acknowledgement

This drawing is made by Arvie Silvano Buenaflor

It is my pleasure to acknowledge: Arvie Silvano Buenaflor, my nephew for this very nice drawing, thank you very much. <u>I Thank you and appreciated for that Good Job!</u>

PLEASE READ THIS BOOK I HAVE THE STORY ABOUT THIS PARTICULAR PICTURE.

A long time ago in the Village there was a boy named Enrique who loved flowers. Anything he planted burst into bloom. Up came flowers, bushes, and even big fruit trees as if they by magic! Everyone in the valley loved flowers too. They planted them everywhere, and the air smelled like perfume. The King Cabisa Eping loved birds and animals, but flowers most of all, and he tended his own garden every day.

But the King Cabisa Eping is very old; he needed to choose a successor to the throne. Who would his successor be? And how would the King Cabisa Eping choose? Because the King Cabisa Eping loved flowers so much, he decided to choose the flowers. First, the next day a proclamation was issued: all the children in the villages were to come to the King Cabisa Eping palace. There they would be given special flower seeds by the king Cabisa Eping.

"Whoever can show me their best in a year's time, will succeed me to the throne," he said. This news created great excitement throughout the villages, children from all over the Villages community swarmed to the King Cabisa Eping palace to get their flower seeds. All the parents wanted their children to be chosen the King Cabisa in the Village, and the children hoped they would be chosen too!

When Enrique received his seed from the King Cabisa Eping, he was the happiest child of all. He was sure he could grow the most beautiful flower. Enrique filled a flowerpot with rich soil. He planted the seed in it very carefully. He watered it every day. He couldn't wait to see it sprout, grow, and blossom into a beautiful flower!

Day after day passed, but nothing grew in his pot. Enrique was very worried. He put new soil into a bigger pot. Then he transferred the seed into the rich black pot. Another two months he waited. Still, nothing happened. By and by the whole year passed.

Spring came, and all the children put their best clothes to greet the King Cabisa Eping in the Village Palace. They rushed into the village with their beautiful flowers, eagerly hoping to be chosen. Enrique was ashamed of his empty pot. He thought the other children would laugh at him because for once he couldn't get a flower to grow.

His clever friend ran by, holding a great big plant! "Enrique!" he said. "You're not really going to the King Cabisa Eping with an empty pot, are you? Couldn't you grow a great big flower like mine? I've grown lots of flowers better than yours," Enrique said. "It's just this seed that won't grow."

Enrique's father overheard this and said, you did your best, and your best is good enough to present to the King Cabisa Eping. Holding the empty pot in his hands, Enrique went straight away to the King Cabisa Eping. The King Cabisa Eping, was looking at the flowers slowly, one by one. How beautiful all the flowers were! But the King Cabisa Eping was frowning and did not say a word.

Finally, he came to Enrique; Enrique hung his head in shame, expecting to be punished. The King Cabisa Eping asked him, "Why did you bring an empty pot?" Enrique started to cry and replied, "I planted the seed you gave me, and I watered it every day, but it didn't sprout. I put it in a better pot with better soil, but still, it didn't sprout! I tended it all year long, but nothing grew. So today I had to bring an empty pot without a flower. It was the best I could do."

When the King Cabisa Eping heard these words, a smile slowly spread over his face, and he put his arm around Enrique. Then he exclaimed to one and all, I have found him! I have found the one person worthy of being the King in the Village. Where you got your seeds from I do not know, for the seeds I gave you had all been cooked. So it was impossible for any of them to grow. I admire Enrique's courage to appear before me with the empty truth, and now, I reward him with my entire Villages and make him the King of all the Village community. Welcome Enrique, you are the successor to the throne in the Village.

LIVING MY DREAMS

This picture is my original home from when I was young

INTRODUCTION
LIVING MY DREAMS

Dreams do come true! Wow! My belief in the secret dreams will grow stronger if you actually see the tick marks in your diary to accomplish on all the things that you wanted to do and have it. Life is truly lovely phenomenal. I am living at this time was once my dreams to discover the purpose. Stay up to date with your dreams, bigger and better than could be reasonably expected of the most desired in your life that never likely to be. You're about to face the biggest period of luck in your life, but since you did not follow your dream? Try watch out! Suns out, bugs out! Getting caught up in your dreams is your natural form of self-expression.

You don't have to imagine a new life of prosperity, because you are not prepared it is about to change, to reveal and to discover for your dreams comes true, is the powerful belief offers an endless amount of positive thinking, and only a few of the many dreamers have fantastic results. Everything points to you getting everything you've ever wanted and more. Finally, you can start to get constant prayers for your dreams and follow the direction everything points to you getting rich you ever wanted and more. Walking my dreams come true this morning just as the sun came up, something struck me that I could hardly wait to share, I was dreaming that I already made a schedules to go around the world with no stopping, on beautiful days, a lot of money, I always begin my morning with a brisk walk in the garden, breathing in the fresh air deeply and taking stock of the magnificent nature surrounding me.

Living my dreams is a person of action and not one of empty words or promises. You take a down-to-earth approach to showing others how you emphasize with and care about each other. You are a person of dreams convictions dedicated to making sure your family members and friends are happy and well cared for. You like to make sure your desk is in order, your house is clean, and your obligations are being caught up. When you can't have your affairs in order, and your dreams can't come true, it makes you nervous. You work to be the nuts and bolts that keep the good machine of life working properly.

As being a Filipina, I feel that it would be beneficial and inspiring to all the Filipino's to read my book, not only a Filipino's but to all the people young and old. If you believe in dreams! Do come true. Are you one Of the Millions of people who dream to get rich? Have you tried to wonder how to get them? You have done all the works, and now it is time to show the world that you really following your dreams and had come true. You look at your new creation like a frog wanted to become a king and the frog became one. But, have you really thought about how the world will get to see the Frog became a king? Don't worry you are not alone. There are countless thousands, even millions of dreamers that have not really cracked their goals. There are many who have dreams to be somebody and get rich still struggling. However, I am guessing they got a little out of each dream they did not follow enough to continue the dream that is about to change their life that they needed. Your life can change and your prayers one by one can all be answered, even though the grace of God is granted only to some help us bare the Daily hardships of life for the love of God. Grant us courage and the perseverance to fight the good fight and that the merciful Savior will be with us in our final hour on earth. Teach us to be generous like living our dreams will come true so that we may use our talents and energy for self-discipline and may lead us to become an excellent person by following our dreams would come true.

The Forgotten Dreams is the powerful dreams of self-discovery. There was nothing to change, either my dreams were good or my dreams were bad, but thinking makes it so real, sharing many things to talk about our own radiant moments of revelation on the good dreams path is very remarkable. It shows clearly how was the beginning of the awaken dreams because you owe to be happy, building your own thinking and there sometimes you laugh when you remember what was it? It was good! You think sometimes, you want to be a king or a queen, and you became one. Each challenge becomes an opportunity for truth. Don't be afraid of promises, once we are engaged in the good dreams planning, take care that plan think and remember it will become an opportunity for growth.

When I was young, I chose to be a businesswoman. I want to travel abroad. I don't know anybody in faraway places, like America. But my awaken dreams were telling me to go for it, success is your birthright. When you empower your awaken dreams, it will not lose the love and the unique gifts that you are going to give of yourself is the first reconciled to your own happiness. You are the light of your dreams, a love that is set on the heart cannot be taken whoever wants to empower your thought one mile, go with two. You should love your neighbor and hate your enemy, BUT!

"According to the HOLY BIBLE by THE GIDEONS, Matthew Chapter 5, verse, 44, 45 and 46 But I say to you, love your enemies, bless those who curse you, do good to those who hate you, and pray for those who spitefully use you and persecute you." "That you may be sons of your Father in Heaven; for He makes His sun rise on the evil and the good, and sends rain on the just and the unjust." "For if you love those who love you, what reward can you have? Do not even the tax collectors do the same?"

Then fasten your love Catcher around your heart and get ready to attract all the dreams and the good luck are destined to come.

Feelings are so important, I want to talk about my experience, living my dreams, it gives me the courage to release all my fear and allow myself to be strong lifted up to the next stage of life and the fulfillment of my education. My parent doesn't like I will go to college, but I tried myself to find ways how to get it. I was a working student until I graduated with my Bachelor of Science in Education, at Southwestern University Cebu City Philippines; with a major in Mathematics and Minor in English. I became who I wanted in my life. I have a position upon graduation to teach at Tanjay College, for one year and transfer to Madridejos High School for one year, and right after the closing of the classes, a vacation came. During that period of time, I got marriage abroad to Hawaii. I continued my studies in Hawaii, taking Merchandising of Business Admin. I graduated, got a degree, I taught Algebra at Kauai High School, and continued studies for my Master Degree Business Admin at the University Of Phoenix. I also worked at Liberty House department store, taking care of nine departments as a department manager for fifteen years. I do living my dreams. I have a dream to become an author of a book up until now, I still writing I love for many things especially the current passions, always been the coolest things which are most beautiful in life. So, I love my dreams deeply incredibly much more than before, that I had found a way to write a book and come back to read again. I fear that being a Filipino I cannot write my story good but, I know I will go through. There are no words to express my fighting moment for this project, and I am at a loss for words. So, I love my dreams. I followed my dreams and had come true. I was nervous, but I did not let that stop me from writing a book. This is my number two books, and I am about to start for my number three. I had worked and remembered all those dreams seemed like a far-fetched dream and now I am living that dreams. It's time to release those doubts and fears. Finally, you can start to get a constant result from your dreams go true.

Take Action Today and Get the Results You Deserve for Tomorrow!

Make advancements in your job or career by uncovering the hidden strengths inside of you, then learning how to use them for success; I have a couple of jobs. I became a nurse aide, and tax preparer   I am currently working. I could share this information with the decision of my own life. I have already mentioned, only you can decide what your life will be like. I suggest you value each day of your life experience so.; you have the wisdom to turn out and get the strength and hope to accomplish what you started. Discover develop and master new talents you probably don't even know you have! I wish you to find the good balance of wit and strength in your life. I will give you advice work on the edge of your capabilities. You will find that it is not as difficult as it may seem to be, but the result of such work cannot be the same or compared to anything else what you do. Gain crystal-clear awareness of your hidden talents, inner skills, and natural abilities so you can take advantage of previously hidden opportunities for success! Naturally, begin attracting more harmonious rewarding and long-lasting love into your life. Live joyfully in the moment more than ever understanding your deepest inner motivations, ambitions, needs, wants and desires. Learn how to deal with, understanding, and influencing, your family, friends, lovers, employers, and employees. Discover a simple quick way to maximize your energy and reduce your stress; the future is in your hands once you can see the map of your destiny.

You know you made your best. Those were the recipes of the best wonderful education. Today you worry, and tomorrow you will be happy. We all have a tendency to underestimate our power; the fear of failure is nothing more than a state of mind. We must think positively and think successfully have no fear of failure. I always remembered my parent precept and imagined one's own big family; for some of us, it is God, for others their families and friends. Will it be a constant fight or reasonable compromise with family and yourself, it's up to you to decide. You have to bring your principles into your life, no matter who you will be in the future and what your life will be like, but always remember your family first, where you came from. Act boldly and enthusiastically, make a commitment to your plan of action. That's what I did, living my dreams.

We cannot let go of the past. I woke up early the next morning, and I wondered, but, everything the same as it was, I can't understand and feel the stiffness in the left side back of my body. I thought, what happens to me? I hadn't turned over because I slept well, after every dream and every dream. I had remembered the way walking, and follow my dreams the easy laughter and conversation came to my imagination. Consider all the alternatives how sweet above the dreams, then kiss me, a kiss to build a dream on, is the interest of love before it comes due. If you think you can handle without interest, then go right ahead wait for two more days one is yesterday, and the other is tomorrow.

The reason is if you cannot do it at all then change your original thoughts, and maybe you can change the world. Yes, walking and follow my dreams is a beautiful one for everybody's thought, we need to appreciate that tough our irreplaceable and priceless life and of course we can utilize the time every day in just a few minutes each day thinking works wonders for our mind. Simply, thinking, dreaming, and planning is not enough we must do knowledge and power. Applied the knowledge is a power and action is the key to think about, what it is, You know, it was my experience everything that you can see in this world worthwhile in life comes to us free really, our minds, hearts, eyes, moon, world, tonight, cry, one, bodies, souls, intelligence, love, dreams, sweet, time, life, thing, go, tell death though us part, aspirations, and ambitions are all walking and follow my dreams. They are all LOVE!

If you engage or start a new love, it takes courage, and trust self- confidence to go through, and the most important hurtful feelings about first love is when you break up, and still thinking until both of you contemplating dreams of love life in the context of the history of your own teaching, and particularly focusing on the difficulties, and finding the solution. Both of you, as it may seem slack of unity, but the result of this inspirational love have been considered, the most truly crucial for the first time, in the history of your love life is to forgive each other. It will be the point issues of your true love story, the beginning and the end of the new era, and this is the answer spoken by your own dreams. Really, such a breakthrough; don't give up, respect and love each other.

But chances are! You are asking for a second chance. Let the true love hold your hands and guide you down the love life path of your dream. Focus on your dreams and desires but then all the day to day drama kicks in. Your dreams have a very real element of knowledge and commitment of changing to the truth. Think of your dreams, love it every minute, learned the arts of love daring to be yourself, graduate from your studies is the great gifts of deep inspiration from your dreams. As I said before, you have to follow your dreams and live with it.

Is your life not going in the direction you want? Do you wonder where your relationships, job, and finances will be three to five years from now? I can use my dreams to answer those questions, so you can take charge of your life and understand your future. If we remembered those days in our lives the natural creation of nature, a fascination and creation of the world are all in its movement. We have seen change in nature nothing stays the same. The ocean has low tide and high tide, there are nights and days, emerge as the sun rises. The morning glory splendid shows the beauty of the beautiful flowers. Imagine reading a guide that will tell you day-by-day what will happen to you during the next two years of your life. Wouldn't it be wonderful to no longer have to worry about what tomorrow has in store for you because you'll know in advance? I will even outline the four biggest challenges I will face in my life. When you are prepared for challenges, you can overcome them. That's the power of dreams. There are pinnacles coming up in life where you will need to make life altering decisions.

It comes immediate effects is more enduring result is a greater freedom of love. Eventually, hearken unto the lesson that dreams of love bring us, a course correction that will enhance our quality of living. Breaking the law of love makes the deepest tears harboring subconscious patterns that defeat happiness.

I knew for the fax it was my experienced during my time, the stress of loving your education the meetings and fulfillment to thousands of things to be finished to endorse them on time. But, those thoughts have been motivated me to continue my education and finished up of where I was left.

One of the greatest love this world I knew, it is the way of saying "I love you." I love myself, I love what you are doing, I really love you finished your education, I love your idea, I love living my dreams, I love my neighbors, I love my car, I love my family, and brought peace, of my own thought and at the same time walking and follow my dreams.

I knew, I was thinking, and wanted to say the power lies in my own mind and dreams. Make no mistake that this is the process that God created us to love each other and to love him too. Also, we need to engage not just our hearts, but souls and minds as well as in our love for God. We should use our creative power of love to be the attorneys of our own prosecution and to be love, telling feature of a delusion is unlikely dreams of reality to ourselves. When you feel ready, open your eyes and bring yourself back to reality, You may want to note down anything that you can remember about your dreams meditate and remain in this state of deep contemplation for a little while longer, note any thoughts or images that float into your mind, don't censor them, just be aware of the dreams they are messages from your love.

LOVE ME WITH ALL OF YOUR HEART BY "Engelbert Humperdinck"

Love me with all of your heart, that's all I want to love. Love me with all of your heart or not at all, just promise me this, that you'll give me all your kisses, every winter, every summer, every fall, when we are far apart or when you're near me, love me with all of your heart as I love you, don't give me your love for a moment, or an hour, love me always as you've loved me from the start, with every beat of your heart!!! Just promise me this, that you'll give me all your kisses every winter, every summer, every fall, when we are far apart or when you're near me, love me with all of your heart as I love you, don't give me your love for a moment or an hour, love me always as you've loved me from the start with every beat of your heart.......

LOVE is a Many Splendored Things

Love Word Cloud

I know, everything in life is love! When I never would have imagined LOVE is LOVE the benefit is the beautiful love, the absolute freedom, the peace of mind when you say I love you, that's the amazing highest word on earth. "God is Love." Love is an ongoing receiver to another heart that wants to confide in you how much they felt about you. Both loves and dreams are the direct results of our own thought. Most individuals are wishing and hoping to be love and dream of their own imagination to be true. Only if both hearts ignite is going to reveal the butterfly into your heart, send you some strange facts about your near future love. Only a few know that a definite plan, plus an unbending thought are the only truth that dependable to commit a deeper love. The decision making of a deeper love and more basically attached to making decisions with the other side of the brain. The correlation of a thinking process that is approved by the decision, by reason, by logic, and by the rigidity of your brain and to love that means of assuring your true love for success. The greatest thought of love you can ever dream. Remember how you used to be scared of things as a kid, but if you love to do those certain things as a kid and continue to do all the way until you got older; then you are no longer scared. Same deal here, just get out and start doing you can make up all the excuses in the world. I now have every reason to think that this love is a many splendored things is just on the road for everybody the celestial prompted confirmation of the individual to involve, and action needed to be taken as soon as possible. I can tell you now you can't imagine how happy you are going to be in deciding to listen to your brain and follow to your dreams and do not listen to your heart, that, you can decide later, when your Angel is going to reveal to you some strange facts about your love in the future. Maybe not the way we think but the way we perform and considering love is in paradise overcoming their challenges to follow their dreams and live the life they want. This is what I called, "Living my dreams."

DID YOU KNOW? THAT THERE ARE FIVE LOVE LANGUAGES?

The five different kinds of love languages are:

1. Verbal and non-verbal, are words of affirmation
2. Always have quality time together
3. Give and Receive, receiving gifts from each other
4. Acts of Services, ask for help or help each other
5. Physical touch, have known a number of other loving couples of whom are entertainers act and earns a love.

Will, if you know, good, then you are expert. If you do not know yet, let me tell you, as we grow a human, we start to realize that the number one most natural thing that we crave for in life is love. Love is a deep feeling of attraction that keeps us going every day in life, and helps us shape our personalities by becoming the person that we are today. So, in order to help humans know what kind of love they crave and know where to get it from, a Christian family counselor and the author came up with the five love languages.

Love languages are: as I mention above verbal and non-verbal communications between couples which improve the mental and physical well-being of both partners. These mutual expressions and actions help to build up a nurturing environment in which couples can improve both their emotional and physical intimacy levels. The five different languages are words of affirmation, quality time, receiving gifts, acts of service, and physical touch. Each represents the different ways that people get turned on by, based on their personalities and interest. And after all the survey was the majority of a loving couple, they both agreed that the best interest of them has, a quality time together. It told them their love language has a good quality time together both of them where ever and forever. Because you will know, what do you think is going on?

People that have the love language of the quality time view the undivided attention of the person that they are affectionate about as a way of saying. "I really, really, really, really love you!" It's very critical to physically be there and support that person one on one to make them feel loved. These tend to feel truly special and loved like at times like dinner when the TV is off, the utensils are down, and all chores and tasks are on standby. But when there are distractions, postponed dates, or the failure to listen is present, these the quality time people can be especially hurt and feel hated.

Another one what was the result of the survey has enough to truly believe that the love language has the quality time after they knew each other and introduced to their own characteristics. It is just natural to do things like they were on autopilot because the body loves to have quality time. Talking to a friend face to face instead of texting or wanting to people understand that the problems through listening to each other. For that, they were experiencing a boy wanting to hang out with their friend. Trying to have a conversation with their lovers and understanding what's going through. Ability is what you're capable of doing it. Motivation determines what you do. Attitude is how well you do it. You must expect great things of yourself before you can do them.

Therefore, always makes an effort to do things together on a day they were available, take the most priority to spend time with. It would be a hundred percent believe that this person and this really likes getting to know each other very well. You know after getting that feeling certainly, they crave it so much, that if they were to see this handsome self somewhere around the school, they will attempt to go through a route where they would cross each other's paths. Just knowing that someone would want to go out of their

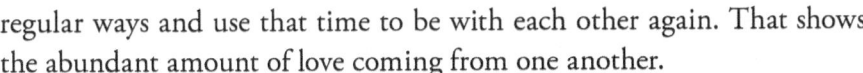

regular ways and use that time to be with each other again. That shows the abundant amount of love coming from one another.

But on the other hand, if someone does the opposite, that doesn't turn them on. If you notice, that they got super angry, when a guy says that he likes someone else, through text, but barely wants to hang out with you after that, like they don't even try to talk to you when he passed by you, and on top of that, if a guy were to flirt with somebody else? I know that this is not the true love of legitimate action what is needed is to learn the drama now. Ready to understand that by loving and staying until the thunder boomed in the distance faint but powerful and both of the lover's dreamers knew it was time to break and leave without notice. But the most important part of their love is the heartbreak for each other. But, if they paid attention to the details of their dreams, then little things will remain in love especially when they practice to respect with each other. Something important thing in your lives be forgiveness to each other, don't be overextending to yourself turn a flow of love into a dream, developed a system that goes the ultimate message of love. And the youthful romance is a model of the innocence of love and positive thinking it's not always convincing, their emotional love and dream interaction. Therefore, occasionally peril possible inappropriate for the teen young lovers who are not well grounded in their love. They must tighten its grip on each other is you do your own thing what you enjoy, what is fun and what comes easily to you for what is good at it. Success and happiness is a matter of allowing yourself and building of what you find, each one of us was born to be a star in something very special.

That is the way you grow chances are the dreams will continue to guide you if you believe in all walks of life.

Those people who love to do the most works will find the most time; the advances of the true value of time to enjoy every moment of it. Sometimes you will never find time for anything, but if you want time to yourself you must make it. Remember a dream will come true if you put the responsibility on it. The most precious thing on dreams can give you a lifetime of happy memories, and you have to write your own records of what you are dreaming, if you fail to control your own mind you have to be sure you will not control somebody else but only you, they are a way of life.

I totally agree! The trouble is I have my dreams pretty sweet, I travel abroad which I did not imagine; I will be going to Hawaii. When I was young, I had a good job that paid really well. I was a teacher at Madredejos Provincial High School, Madredejos, Bantayan, Island, Cebu, Philippines; government employees were paid really well and gave me freedom (however it's within the wrong time and place that doesn't really resonate with my dreams or passions) lovely little town, great friends, students, and co-teachers.

My fear was to take a jump in a job that is not for me because going back and forth at home a fear of riding a small boat to go and transfer from island to island was not comfortable for me. However, I dream of every single day, I feel that it's not sitting quite right, I am far away from my family, my parents, always wrote me a letter come home this weekend, we miss you or we have something gathering, I need to break the routine and discover my full potential to actually step back outside my comfort zone again. Anyway, I live my dream, I've trusted my heart it's not let me down, but always follow your dreams, and it will come true. If you were an adventurer person; please follow your dreams, challenge it do not fear change, and do not fear new places and people. Always act as if you were the most successful person on earth give inspiration and motivation for loving your dreams come true. Let each of us become all that we are capable of being in love; nobody but ourselves in a world which is doing its best, "DREAMS."

Your dreams are important so dream big with other girls in front of you, even though he told you prior that likes you, gets you straight up pissed off and the feeling of not wanting to talk to that person anymore, not even he is sorry, or a hug could help them. This start to feel hated, and not important anymore which helped you figure out that your love language is truly quality time because you need it.

To me, this assessment has really helped the young teenager to understand the meaning of love. Why are they doing this? And why they feel the certain ways of loving like this? About various things that have happened to those young teenagers, in the past; the loving quality was sacred because they believed that it builds intimacy and trust in a romantic relationship which is something that is going to overcome as we get older. Did you just do that? Smile, even do angry take the test perfect, 100% hundred present, love examination work for the lovers.

Now, that we know our love language, you probably give it as a heads up to the people that you love to show that this is a way for them to love them more and communicate with them better. But, for the heads up, for me, I have to also figure out what kind of love language each of the people that love inhabits to help the communication to them better. Could it be quality time, acts of service, receiving gifts, physical touch or words of affirmation? The only way I can truly find out is by observing how they deal with love and having them take the love languages survey. So if you're really interested, what could be your love of others languages.

The awareness of experience and discovered the power of right to choose would be in yourself. We are the boss of our own self always bigger than our circumstances. There is nothing to be compared in yourself but only you. I discovered, what I was thinking about? I wondered, and I remembered way back from my college life. The memory of my love is forever a true love was dim. As I began to think about it, I had a chance to practice the things I love before. I remember that any given day or life was working busily to do seizing the day to do my worked studies myself, and developed in getting my start in love life, a little fun play while I am young. But, it was far beyond the scope and limits of my own experience. The connection and love relationship remains inactive.

The achievement of your dream love life was so engaging, used your dreams and thought of love to be good. It will get better and better don't limit the opportunities, see what you can do from your hidden dreams. It is about matters how you get there because you cannot win a game, if you do not play. Simply to survive, go, play and follow their policy.

This gesture represents all your desires and dreams being offered up to a loving and generous Universe that is all too happy to turn them into reality. When you are satisfied with your dreams to come true, bring your attention back to yourself imagine that dreams.

Nothing is beyond our reach; nothing is impossible, nothing can stop the rivers flow, nothing can stop the birds flying and never agree that limitation is true, go for it, skies is the limit.

The only freedom which deserves the love and dreams is that of pursuing our own good in our own ideas and efforts to obtain our dreams goals.

"Make yourself familiar with the one you love most." "Behold and beloved frequently in your dreams."

"For without being love she or he will act differently." "Give courage to change the things you can."

"The knowledge of dreams to know the difference" "Always challenge the opportunity for growth."

I have a dream

YOUR LOVE IS BETTER THAN MINE, MY MIND WILL THINK OF YOU ALWAYS; SO I WILL LOVE YOU FOREVER, AND I HOPE YOU WILL DO THE SAME.

Bring your dream renovation to love life by tapping into your love life education goals, maintain your dream focus and remove distractions make your dream a channel of your peace.

I believe my love was great and my dreams turn my minds into a good direction of possibility thinking a potential course of success. Perhaps, the impossible becomes possible dreams; remember we create our own destiny. It's up to you to follow the way the stars guide you. The sun shines, and we feel happy and all of the sudden the rain comes, and suddenly a huge foggy.

Do you believe that the positioning of the stars at the time of your birth influence your personality? Performing this short and simple connection ceremony of the stars will help you to get the best from your dreams desired, if you can remember all in about 5 minutes, those dreams are good so much better when you don't forget your entire dream. Concentrate on your breathing for a few. So, I gaze on you in my memory to see your strength in reality. Pretend you're happy when you're blue, it isn't very hard to do, and you'll find happiness without an end, whenever you pretend. Remember anyone can dream, and nothing's as bad as it may seem, the little things you haven't got could be a lot if you pretend, you'll find a love you can share one you can call all your own, just close your eyes she'll be there, you'll never be alone, and if you sing this melody, you'll be pretending just like me, the world is mine it can be yours my friend, so why don't you pretend. This is the songs by: "Nat King Cole."

Love is a vital principle of happiness:

Moments gradually allowing your dreams to become deeper and deeper in love; then when you feel really relaxed imagine yourself in a beautiful landscape like this picture below it could be beside the sea or up in the mountains it really doesn't matter. Those who will accomplish great things in life are those who are willing to do and discipline their lives and maintain their dreams come true. The sign is cheerfulness, and the dream is the condition of wisdom. The amazing fact is that most lovers plan for everything in their lives except to change their lifestyle to accomplish their goals, and not enough to be love where they wanted it should be.

When the enthusiasm goes out of your life; you do not have too much left, and your dreams becomes dull, and the goals will be lost in your desire. You have to do something that is worth more than the time required to be ready time and effort to accomplish it. Dreams big; loving big; living big; and inspired big; challenge and deep satisfaction in the achievement of love.

I have a dream

The Golden Valley: This drawing made by:Arvie Silvano Buenaflor, Dobdob, Badian, Cebu, Philippines

Living My Dreams
There are two kinds of dreams
The sleeping dreams, and the awaken dreams

We all dreams we all recognize our dreams, as a time of sleeping, a time to think for ourselves and make the better choose the best of all for tomorrow. How did you feel right after the good dreams, feeling better, worst or what? Some people have a hard time understanding or responding to that question. A sleeping dream is a succession of images the mind's emotions and sensation that occur during the stages of heavy sleeping. And the awaken dreams are the promises to your heart and mind to build a dream on in your imagination.

To understand a dream, start by considering your first good feelings on waking by a dream from it. When we say good feelings, we would include our body sensations and energy level. Let our mind and heart guide us on what were the dreams going on and start analyzing the meaning of that certain dream, and that will tell you whether it is good or bad. The reflection of a dreams messages whether positive or negative, what was the reaction to your first feelings. How do you usually deal with your feelings? What fears have held you from acknowledging these feelings? Do you have the strength to follow your heart if it guides you in a different direction or a different path of feelings? Or is it frightening or with goose bumps dreams and happy endings?

As we recall an amazing dream, the moment you move into boldly working toward the fulfillment of your dreams will bring you to the fullness of joy. What are your memories hopes, dreams, desires & fears? Miracles, and how, I wonder, will these dreams end? I don't think so; it literally is a matter of survival.

I'm worried! Why are you denying yourself happiness? You are so close to reaching your dream goals!

Of course, you already know that you're life will be better if your dreams come true as an act of powerful and perfect potential in life. I just wanted to write you and tell you that I love my dreams! I wish I had known how to do the awaken dreams before, but now, what's out. What would you be doing differently?

We always thought we were meant to live a better life and we think we were right. Perhaps no better time than always know there was something greater for you out there. We've sensed something missing in our life, and that there has been a block in our path to getting all that we desire and deserve in the future.

And of course, maybe, we were so right. Throughout our life, some people will say, you couldn't have it all. But deep down in life despite how you may have felt, I'm certain that you always knew you could and should have it all, and now, you can start yourself on that path to living your dream the amazing life you've always wanted it now. Everyone wants to be a winner in the game take responsibility for what happens to the result of the game, and the losers make excuses and blame their partners or someone else. Chances are it was in the midst of those other pressures that the winner of the game love is the big dreamers that knew how to handle the game. So, dream big, set goals, and take action. I knew I had to be one of them. I had won my dreams and jobs I had held, I knew instinctively that none of us was special enough to set up goals. They are always making progress the winners look to the future losers look to the past. On the other hand, happens to them winners tend to be highly in their own ability to control their dreams. It is our mean attitude toward events, is not the events themselves which we can control. Make sure that the dreams you choose are the one you enjoy.

JUMPING INTO A BIG DREAM

The ultimate hope, strength, courage, and awareness are the complete receipt of instant lights. The great lesson learned from the dream will come true is that you have to be patience, perseverance, stick to the point that you have to do it the unflagging courage essential qualities. Treat your dreams a workable lovable and valuable thinking that your dreams will come true, do not underestimate the power of persistence. Everybody has dreams, I can see the story from your eyes, and the night begins to shine, it required attention to weak up activate a dual motion of works. The only greatest weaknesses for everybody or maybe not for all were lies in giving up the most certain way to succeed is to always try just one more time. You will easily develop your own powers and capabilities to do things happen, and you will overcome the goals of any tormenting doubts in your love lifestyle. You will create the best and perfect an unusual performance of your lifestyle a faith that will inspire you and those who are around you, especially your own family, friends, and relatives. Otherwise, you will not be doing it well or fully successfully in your dream big set goals take action.

YOUR DREAMS ARE IMPORTANT, SO DREAM BIG!

Like a deluxe vacation somewhere on beautiful sunny beaches!

Life is a journey, you were born to win, but to be a winner, you must plan to win, prepare to win, and expect to win. The amazing story behind your dreams, it will shock you that your dreams will come true. Let me congratulate you on having such a good believer an old and noble soul before we start dreaming; we have to think and study of what is good for us this dream big is started from our minds promises to use all the knowledge and wisdom to achieve a future solid result.

I can tell that from the day we were born Life wasn't easy for us. But the last thing we should do, is to blame our self for all the hardship and misfortune that we've experienced, the way it works, is that those of us who are a dreamers, always have it harder in our current lives, "we understand" I will explain it more in greater way or great detail as we continue with this dreams reading.

However, for now, I want you to know, that all of us have dreams. The experience goes directly to our mind and heart. It has been said that dreams are the closest thing we can have the emotion to influence the energy to a universal language. Dreams aren't subjective or emotional vibrations of our heart. This goes both ways, like flying a tough time in your dreams suggests that someone or something is stopping you from moving to the next step in your life. Being afraid of flying, you might be having trouble keeping up with the highest goals you promise for yourself. It is a job for your conscious to figure out and implies that you are lacking of confidence within yourself.

The awaken dreams are vivid and convincing dreams about the subjects you are often thinking. These are always performing every time in mind. Classic examples, like: I want to become rich in the future, I want to build my dream home, I want to travel all around the world. I want to win a lottery, and you really win it. In a study of a real dreamer may turn into a reality. That is one in which the dreamer may start to wonder if they are really headed into the right or correct conclusion. I will cleanse my mind by dreaming something that I want, this sound at least once a week, or every other night, I can handle it,

So it will constantly keep the negative spirits away and my surroundings free from any unwanted entities. Sometimes we need to stand up and declare what we want. Always Follow your Dreams! What is the gift here? Just follow you will see the way out. They think that I was asking them to stand before a firing squad, but it is not a firing squad, it is an inspiring love; a dream exercise in giving and receiving love. But part of that in our mind is so afraid of being in love. Learned how to remember whether or not to make a certain love you can.

This is like the song by: Victor Wood
You are my reason to live
All I own I would give
Just to have you adore me.

Till the Moon deserts the sky,
Till all the seas run dry
Till then I'll worship you,
Till the tropic sun grows cold,
Till this young world grows old,
My darling, I'll adore you.

You are my reason to live,
All I own I would give,
Just to have you adore me,
Till the rivers flow upstream,
Till lovers cease to dream,
Till then I'm yours, be mine.
This is according to the song by: Victor Wood

If anyone ever tells you your dreams are silly? Remember there's a millionaire walking straight Who invented the pool Noodles, and focused on blessing of his own desire for peace for the highest interest. Your dreams and mind will tell you that you Can live like this!
But, your love life cannot. It is about to blow out and Your mind it's going to explode.

You must realize that at some point you must perform and must convert those dreams into realities. I was fortunate that my love and dreams taught me a wise adage, actions speak louder than words. You must do a worked long and harder to try to convince your love eventually you must do the knowledge and power dreaming and planning are not enough. You can reflect think dream and plan all that you want, but you also must do the knowledge.

The doers are the happier and successful people are figuring out a way to accomplish who are the people that can say yes. I believe there is a price tag on people who are the genius determination in life.

And because they believe that, they actively make things happen and the competition and the aspirations ultimately drive the kind of experiences they want to have and become accountable to themselves if they are willing to pay the price that is responsible for them.

The mind is a creature of habit' Control of the mind through the power of will is not difficult. Control comes from persistence and Habit at all it's all in the state of mind.

The mark of the dreams comes true.

"DREAM, DREAM, DREAM"

A man walking and follow his dreams

WALKING AND FOLLOW MY DREAMS

THE STORY OF THE OLDEN DAYS

Many years ago, I had been walking on a sweet path for years and follow my dreams, I'm not so sure of where I was going and all of the sudden a sweet path had split confusing. The primary functions of the sweet path are to follow the instructions. So, I study and learned based on proven psychological and metaphysical dream techniques and timeless principles for success. Most of these ideas and thoughts are the interpretation of the dream or concepts of brilliant thinkers, and feel privileged to have the opportunity to invest the wonderful thoughts by walking and following the beautiful dreams.

So, what the heck! What Was That? A sweet path had split confusing? Last night, I had a dream I was walking, and the sweet path had split descended into a cave. The Engkanto and Enrique as someone with dissociative identity disorder and two ladies personalities were all fighting for control in the valley. At the single house Enrique adducts, a young woman and a reign of psychological terror ensues which is the source of the golden valley's river.

The power of accurate dreams and imagination is never-ending. We can see things that are following the beautiful dreams, wants and will always want and probably never get. But it doesn't stop from wanting and wanting to try to accomplish those beautiful things. What have you really got, if not your dreams, then you have not just said the things you truly dream, and say it clear and state the case of which you certainly not the real positive dreams, true enjoyment comes from activity of the mind's creativity and more, much more than this, I did it my way. So, reach your dream goals inch by inch everyday investing the main concerns have been focused on the negativity that is currently blocking you. The fear of this is a bad energy will create resistance and stopping you from achieving your true happiness and to reach your goal of success.

The reflections of positive dreams demonstrate love compassion and point to truly divine destiny. Positive dreams have long conviction through direct experience and provided a decisive proof for everybody's divine destiny encompasses everything. Those dreams have, in fact, and will come that means for what will happen tomorrow, down to the most insignificant event or business or conversation, has already been predetermined. It was my experience some nights in dreams as if I read or think with my eyes and mind, it has happened not long waiting, but perhaps that something I have talked about in dreams, turns out to be true the following day with only a slight interpretation, but, nothing is accidental or coincidental, everything down to the most insignificant events has been destined and predetermined in the mind. I can tell you now that in the present vision dreams changes to a happy and wealthy living are already on the horizon if you follow your dreams will come true.

If you consciously believe that you can't be, do, or have something confusing in your mind, you must claim the strength to continue somehow works out for the best. It will create the circumstances and then expect you to believe it, and find the right way to prove that you are right. You can succeed if you decide to take responsibility for yourself and if you believe that your success is a matter over which you have complete control for yourself. You must have to learn how to program your mind and you will have the key to your own mindset, all I had ever known, my unlimited power lies in my ability to control my thoughts. I'm sure that it has not escaped you the synergy of the meteorites astral skies and planetary action are going to multiply the quotients and combine their

powers to bring about a short but exceptionally opportune to everyone who believes it.

Whenever you are confused, keep heading in the direction that leads towards deepening your love and care for all you seeing, living beings, stopped, including yourself, looked and listened, set in between the two beautiful sweetest paths, and you will never stay far from the path to fulfillment. A confused mind deals within the different direction. Every time we thought were being rejected from something good; I was actually being re-directed to something better. In fact, most of our beliefs have never been tested in the real world of life. Yet, we have lived our whole life basically on the premises that we really believed are true. Do you believe that the positioning of the stars at the time of your birth influences your own personality, character, and happiness? If so, the moment you realize there is a surprising truth behind in the happiest and incredible way.

While waiting for the opportunity of my sweet path at the fork in the road, I have to wish that please make my sweet path last a lifetime warranty of love and beyond. The dream rules are very simple. The roadmap shows you how to find out exactly where your dreams want to go, exactly how to reach your goal of success. I will certainly take good care simple clear-cut set rules and to enjoy a matter over which you have complete control. You know, the mind is a creature of your habit. It thrives upon your dominating thoughts fed it. Through the vision of your will-power, you may discourage the presence of any emotion, and encourage the presence of any other. Control comes from persistence on your mind's habit. It's all in the state of mind and depends upon the quality of your thoughts; if you believed it.

Walking and follow my dreams is a lifetime warranty of love, no amount of determination no amount of willpower and inspiration. It should stay in great condition and sometimes letting your ways of many reproductions. The sweet path will be new every time and all the time. Be smart enough to begin this study of your dream come true as early in your life as a possible accomplishment. Unfortunately, those lifetime warranties of love allow dreams to open up. Just mere days away from that day you dream, the planetary action and power are going to multiply the quotients and combine their power to bring about a short cut power of a big dream; but the exceptionally opportune period for some of us. Why should you really ask? But, I understand this is a legitimate question- and I will try to simplify the true explanation of a dream come true.

Everyone in the Universe is responsible for their own choices and actions of their own life. The most important key to remember when choices or decisions are made is that you do not take it back. Since one cannot turn back the time, one should not be filled with regret in our daily walks of life. When you decide to make a choice, it is at that point that you are willing to accept the consequences or results from that decision. Your guilt will play a factor in an individual's judgment, the cognitive or the emotional experience happens when you realize that you conceded the standards of conduct and morals that bears the weight of why one feels heavy remorse. That is why it is very important to love and live your life the right and good principals in deciding for yourself of what is right and what is wrong. If so ever you go through a life making irrational decisions, will of course later on you be filled with a huge guilt…which will make you believe that you have to do extra to undo the situation that you have gotten yourself into believing.

With all of the obstacles you have been through thus far, but what are the main reasons why you let guilt decide your decisions that are in your lifestyle, or maybe you always been emotional when it comes to your feelings, which you trying to overcome in your daily walks in life. Why do I cry? You know, I have a feeling that I can comprehend in my deepest thoughts that something happen more than bad things coming. If anyone knew that you can find your dream and follow them? I will tell you why I weep. I was hoping my dreams would come true. I am hoping for some sign that would show me the way. But, I think! I did it my way, and end up losing my sweetest journey. But because I was not following instructions, I fear to be unable to handle, I realized I didn't have enough experience. Who is not master of myself? I asked for some support free knowledge for everyone forever, always fun, always unique, always within reach, but it's alright, missions accomplish, it was not the same one as I look the entire sweet path destinations and sometimes our dreams, and treasured develop a big vision. Your astral thought is going to be the host to extremely rare combinations in your planetary thought this puts you in an unusual situation, and consider the privileged to be able to guide a dream come true, if you follow the energy of your dreams, take care of it this offer and instead rely on the chance of a life living. I can tell now that in my visions, changes are already on the horizon.

When I first set onto my sweet path of awakening, to my surprise, the sweet patch had changed. And it was good that I had walked so diligently, all of the sudden for later that very day the pounding footsteps and creaking shoe heels were heard. I fervently pray that no shoe heels damaged would happen. I really felt I should take a second look, as if my walking dreams was a tricked to myself into believing, that I have forgotten the beauty and greatness of my true self, and come to believe that I am not worthy of all the good things and my heart yearns to enjoyed, the journeyed through the assumed walking dream of my mistaken destiny.

The starting point of my mistaken destiny is not to think of making permanent thought the right understanding of what is the difference between possible and impossible. Starting by doing what is necessary to be accomplished first; then do what is possible, and suddenly you are doing the impossible. We thought we could succeed by living up to an image expected by our outer world, but our adaptation has been the dear cost of our inner thoughts. In the attempt to make others believe for something we are not, then, it's a big mistake. You know, when you tell a lie long enough, you begin to believe all the way through. The beautiful journey of today's lie can only believe when you tell the truth, and to let go of yesterday's lie.

To get the best and most out of your dreams, put the best dream in most of your thought into it, and look to this day, for it is important life, the very important life of life. In this day's brief pause lie all the verities and realities in the life of our existence. It is good to stretch the imagination to its breaking point, to play with possibilities. The most important discipline of communion is the practice of simple kindness, and to push the outer limits of our self; but to come down to the nitty-gritty of everyday problem. To develop that hopefully put your dream in its proper perspective, you should calm down, do not follow to a high of your believing too much of a dream. One dream never finds life worth living.

One dream always has to make it worth living. The bliss of every growth, the glory of the most attractive action, the splendor of beauty in everyone's dream, for yesterday was gone and tomorrow is only a big vision of our thought. Dream week up today well lived and makes yesterday a dream of happiness, and tomorrow is a dream of hope. That's why I cry. All is for the best of the best of all possible dreams.

"To dream the impossible dream;" each one of us has the ability to dream the game of thought and mind with balance, harmony, and joy, but we need to know the rules and the principles of positive dreams, negative dreams and right dreams. The truth of the dreamers haven't been afraid in the dark, royal road to the unconscious and tried to travel down that road. The road becomes the mystery of the dark, in the end, it makes the dreamers hope for a better life and happiness from yesterday's thought. Dreams do mean something, and they are universal dreams actually influence with our own behavior. The dreams of the impossible dreams and the dreams of the possible dreams are the reality of truth.

Think of a person who's very happy go lucky, have many children who loved to live in the little golden valley's world. As he lives there, there is no happiness, harmony, and no honey no balance and no real time of love because they keep divorcing or splitting their other half. Be kind to one another, be compassionate to your fair, forgiving to one another, if we are going to live worthy as chosen of your love then adopt a forgiving redemption of happiness. But, there is still that negativity past that you hold onto, which weakens your mindset at times sometimes other opinions influence you to make decisions based on what other's feel. You have to stop living your lifestyle for everyone else. You have to control your own life because no one else will. However, if you noticed that you have a soft spot for people going through times and tend to feel guilty for not doing more to help those who pour their emotions out of you. You have to be careful not to absorb every problem because guilt will keep you in the hole. The best thing in life for other people to become better human beings is to show them, tough love.

When it comes to relationships, it's important to accept that no one is perfect. We all have faults and can improve on being a better person in this Universe. Relationships have its ups and downs. A lot of breakups are due to miscommunication with each other lack of love misunderstanding within the relationships. It's important to everyone do not throw away your second chances out the window. When you are in love, you can go into the relationships like a trial and error, which is a method for solving problems. Those that succeed in love is because they know what they want and they don't give up until their achievements are met. It is important not to let our guilt be a reason why you do something, if you are guilty, into making a decision to help someone else; then it does not hold any value when you make a choice it should be because you are confident and sure of what you want at the time. The same thing applies to help someone else; you should not only want to help because you feel like you have to or, if you do not, you will be feeling remorse, later on, that's a sign of selfishness because you did a good deed for your own personal and emotional needs. And the Universe does not take too kindly to that in deciding to help those who are fortunate than you are supposed to be because you wanted to help.

Of course, you focused on your love desire goals, that's your dreams will come true, by putting yourself in the forefront, you are sending positive energy out into your dreams, and the favor will be returned in blessings that you won't miss because you got to know each other if you pay attention and focused your good relationships on a deeper level, you start to love and understand each other the likes and dislikes. Especially the children eventually get fed up with their action and caring for their families, lack of pleasure and lack of enjoyment of the entire families dreams, and decides to become single. The parents say, you have the ability to be a father or a mother, but you need to understand married life especially the children, whom they can call mom or dad? That's why second chances are important to be considered. Have you ever notice to consider that your mind's idea that your love life reflects the emotion of the true picture of yourself? The same way as your attitude, know that your mind is limitless and that there is nothing to prove the impossible dreams., to dream of the possible dream to accept that you have nothing to lose and the freedom to choose from your thoughts that your dreams would come true, since our mind usually holds only one thought at a time, we must think, positively and sure constructively, the best thought and attitude of well-being do not waste time to say I love You, say it right there your world will really change and you will become the lover's love the kind of lovers would really like to be the best of the bests. The love and respect for you are the most important as far as they are concerned. Give happiness the sign of *I love you,* here is a beautiful *flower* it comes from my loving heart to you from me *I love you,* my honey.

Love

Love   *Love*

Love

The original valley nature of *roses* with illusions and truth about the story of love a second chance lifetime warranty of love, to know that nothing is more than remarkable about the positive dreams, if I give my *heart* to you, will you handle it with care, than given a cost of the negative dreams, will you always treat me tenderly, if I give my *heart* to you, think it over and be sure, that you are able to love me, tell the end of our lifetime warranty of love. This is a genuine love; freedom of my own *heart* and mine a secret love; I do believe you got to take a moment mixing your dreams that dreams would come true, I love my roses and *you.* The rose flower: its meanings and symbolism, the rose is one of the most famous and beloved of all the flowers. As William Shakespeare once wrote "What's in a name?" that which we call a rose by any other name would smell as sweet "Roses have been revered for centuries. Historical evidence shows they were grown in China about 5,000 years ago and they have continued to play a part in history ever since. What does the Rose flower mean? The rose has many meanings which vary depending on its color.

However, any rose can be commonly seen as a symbol of:

- Love
- Honor
- Faith
- Beauty
- Balance
- Passion
- Wisdom
- Intrigue
- Devotion
- Sensuality
- Timelessness

Remember, the difference between the positive dreams and negative dreams, were discussing the concepts in them we all marveled at what we were learning. This is truly revealed the secrets of the true meaning of the negative and positive dreams. But life went on and some people lost track too dearly when acquired at the cost of love. They went on their way to create their own success in the world. The beauty of this touching positive and negative dreams story will captivate the heart of every reader. There was an emotional confusion of a certain smile, and a certain space of a sweet patch has just spoiled the walking dreams. I'm annoyed and overjoyed and still getting confused about why my positive dreams did not perform better than negative dreams.

The walking dreams provided on being in excellent conditions as good in life and have a great time just being alive. It is so good to come back give me all your love your high profile the loving atmosphere are very good young dynamic sweetheart, where you can find me, then activate your love, so you can reach the unreachable star, no matter how far, the Happier you are, and you almost can touch the small package to proves that good things come from afar.

There was thankfulness, and a doubt every night if you have a dream, reveals to be true, but the negative dreams constantly win. After popping my thought, it would be amazing if those dreams will remain to be true. Total mental breakdown, I have a lot of feeling right now, of double thinking are those real? There was a denial seriously; those dreams could have been a secret meaning behind the new day will convince you to never again thanking the series of your thought. But I am actually overjoyed to finally review the thought of my dreams. It was a relief; my positive dreams are really disappointed. I have never felt so conflicted; I hate to dream that I had pretty much forgotten my sweet patch when installing in me the mindset for success that helped me become the person of today.

I hate to dream it again, but no one can predict the future, a secret is to set up the bear to remember and promise to put love into a bargain and kept love at a distance, week up for putting me to ease and forcing awaken trailing and spoiling the walking dreams. But there was something else that made me want to remember a person who is physically fit performs better at any job. Fatigue makes the negative dreams contributor to our minds that you are increasing the greatest chances for a long night sleep. You are a dream, a creator of happiness, an artist who has touched my heart you led me a full life and able to see beauty where others do not. Dreams is a wonder lesson, we could not foresee the future, but then who can? Nobody! There's only freedom which deserves the dreams comes true is that of pursuing our own good, in our own way, so long as we do not attempt to deprive others on their dreams, or impede their efforts to obtain it. The most important thing is to love your dreams and try to remember the story never move while you weaken it; it is wonderful to double check what was the story of the walking dreams. Don't spend a lot of unnecessary time with moving turning around your body, there is a tendency the dreams will go away and your mind will become empty, have the courage to know what you remember in accordance with what you are thinking just follow the walking dreams.

Hopefully, other people will come to understand what the dreams is, that when we enter into this world, we already had a dream, we all do so with two wings. One true dream is the wing of infinite power, connection you with the entire universe, supporting you with the whole support in your life from now to eternity. And the other dream wing, is that witch you have consciously activated, this is the dream wing of action when it does, you will have to fight into the world of unlimited possibilities where anything and everything is being possible for as a human being who is able to understand how truly powerful your dream is, and only then will you understand all it takes within you to create, what is your strong dream desire.

Do these techniques and principles this will really work, I understand and respect your intelligence more than just to tell you that if you have a dreams, catch it right away while you can remember this techniques will works, I really expect you to believe me, because it is based on proven result by my own experience. I can tell you about the positive dreams and the positive results were turning them into inspirational ideas and dreams become reality.

Dreams are what we value, not what we have, that makes us living in a real world, make dreams the old fashioned way, inherit it, not just go to sleep and dream tonight, and no more, but a little more for the lavishing sake, that little more which is worth all the rest. And if you suffer, as you must, wait for your another dream, put your mind into it, that you will be dreaming tonight, and the sky is the limit and clear, then out of your very doubt and happiness will be born the supreme joy of life.

One of the greatest dreams opportunities proverbs is patience and the partnership of wisdom and you never become successful by dreaming, you become successful by working. To be nobody but yourself in a dream which is doing its best, in every night; to make you like everybody else means to fight the hardest fight of your dreams to become reality. You become successful by working to the best of your ability, let everybody practice the art that they know best, having faith in your dreams to reach, your goal of success.

Each one of us has the ability to have a dream, it is good to have a dream and the greatest wealth you can ever get will be in yourself, and there is no wealth but life, we can make ourselves rich by making our dreams come true, but it's up to you how to follow the walking dreams. Life works according to our own principle and physical law. You have your own privileged and formula to have the opportunity for success. Dreaming to be a millionaire is not a bad thing, it will require commitment on your part, just follow the walking dreams.

Be very honest with your dreams and yourself, nobody else is going to see this noble dreams, but only you. It is very simple exercise that most people have never done, which is also a great way to learn more about your dreams. Those traits that you know definitely you have, should mark excellent those that you lack and need. You see, most people believe that based on the definition of your dreams and there is a meaning can give a set of their own traits. However, they then complain that half of the dreams do not apply to them. They think that's a good dream is good enough reason to lose interest or trust in believing. It is a common misconception and I don't want to be people confused about a good dreams.

The truth is that dreams do not help tell you if they really true at the moment, but it will come true in the long run if you really believe. It only tells you who you should become stars and the truth of the stories and the other objects in the universe that constantly interact with each other. If you choose to listen to the dreams that God spirt send you while sleeping, in other words, positive traits are the best version of what you can become, whereas negative traits are the worse version of yourself. This is a direct relation to what a dream is, being a super athlete, you have a great predisposition to become one, but if you are never actually trained, then you will never be good at any sports. Regardless of how good your physical condition or a good dreamer you are.

For example, if you're a good dreamer, and your dream chart strongly indicate that you are helpful and romantic, it doesn't mean that you write everyone a check and then each night you sit under your lover singing him a love song it only means if you want to, you can very easily become a romantic person, because it comes to you naturally! It is your predisposition being romantic, does not require a lot of work for you, even if naturally know how to help other people; does not even automatically mean that you are a dreamer. Now, think about it, because nothing and no one else knows but your own dreams, will come up with amazing solutions and ideas on how to improve your dreams, have a good night sleep and that your dreams will give your brain a puzzle which is very important on how to improve a dream. A promise is a promise there a great insurance of absolute truth and honesty have dramatic effects of the best policy of love; they are the only ones that can do it. Truth and honesty are absolutely the big essential ingredients for promises. Success is the truth in binding their love together creating the love to be learned the true essence of love and dream. Both success and failure are the main terms of results and habit. Failure in your dreams is infinitely much better than those who try to do nothing and succeed and try to remember your dreams don't be it. At the first time you meet each other, you do not know what to make of this strange dream, but soon we being pondered the importance of the dreams come to respect and revere who has given them the new vision to read what's in your mind. Given advice to look at these picture planned to take the world by storm and make something magnificent of their dreams, write a story or read as much as possible, don't limit yourself, It's the author's has strengths and weaknesses, learn as much as your dreams you can do about how to make a good sweetheart, learn how it works, how to get a good relationships, respect each other. How to market your love, who's or which you can look for. How many of them really lived out their dreams? Did they do what they think or what the dreams telling them to accomplish? There's a wealth of information in everybody's mind and, it's important to understand the dreamer's aspects of dreaming to be a lover's love. If you believe both of you like each other, then you have to do something about it, in the process of getting turned away by each other, or both of you are unwilling to forsake your dream desire? Then you need to understand the conventions so-called love me with all of your heart, simply to get the goal, put your love out there and live the truth, the universe will fix and take care of the rest, you can't be a lover if you don't know how to love.

THE GOLDEN VALLEY A DREAM TO REMEMBER

Once upon a time in a distant golden valley, there was a family living magnificent being a fashioned out of a new era and dreams of becoming rich one day and they became one: There is only one family living in the valley no neighbors, no animals, but, there are some other people that, they will not even be associated with other people like us.

On that house, living the King, and the Queen, they have two daughters and one son.

The great king name:	Cabisa Eping
His queen name:	Maria Elina
First daughter:	Maria Choco
Second daughter:	Maria Fely
Brother:	Enrique
Admirer 1st daughter:	Engkanto

Who am I? And how, I wonder. Will this great dreams end? But King Cabisa Eping thinks sometimes a dream to remember, and despite his own acceptance that they were living alone one family in the golden valley with nobody else his dreams had come true. There was a huge golden stone in the valley where they were living near their house. This beautiful magnificent being was fashioned out of tons of pure gold and stood as tall as five men. The golden stone sat serenely in a standing position in the yard behind of their house on a hilltop overlooking a peaceful little golden valley. The great family was playing around together and contemplating the depths of their being. King Cabbisa Eping and Maria Elina, have three children two girls, and one boy, Enrique. The older girl name Maria Choco, and the younger is Maria Fely, they quit being an extra in other people's lives and became the stars of their own, and the whole family became rich.

Then one day a young teenager Maria Choco was sitting on the button of the stone meditating, as she arose she leaned on the stone a little piece chipped off the stone and fell to the ground. To her great surprise, she noticed something shiny underneath the stone. She then ran faster to their house and tell all the family that she discovered there was a golden stone behind our house, come quickly, she shouted, the stone is gold, the stone is gold. When they saw and noticed that Maria Choco was telling the truth, together they were very happy before long all of the façades had been removed the grasses of the golden valley were restored to its original golden beauty.

King Cabbisa Eping said, this is an excellent time to approached the headquarter community around living the golden valley because we were different from them, we have to come out in the light. Before, there were some people were not baptizes by their own religion, but, they still living with us around. In other words, we cannot see them. But they can see us. They have their own places to live. They have their own time to come out. Most likely they come out in the night. Our day is their night and our night is their day. That is why they don't like to see the SUN. They don't like the SUN, they like the night only, and the moon is their light.

I really became a "KING," Cabisa Eping said; and I became one.

This is the one we have been questing for all our life in the golden valley where we live for a long time the goldstone is yours and mine. Before, people told me, how you can think you could succeed by living in the golden valley with no outer world?

But I found my dreams come true. It is important that you understand the meaning of dreams come true. Getting rich you will be surprised how much you have benefited in dreaming without even expecting it.

The thermostat in the golden valley is set as high cold as 120 degrees, as it will go the cold air that will never go away. Years passed, and after time goes by the family became a young teenager, older daughter Maria Choco, has a dream. I can tell you that from the day Maria Choco was born, life wasn't easy for us, we lived in the golden valley no neighbors no stories, No buildings around us, all you can see were the jungles and trees, a cave with plenty of gold inside, ready to transport to the other country to sale them.

You know, the dream story of this was ever grateful for its founder. King Cabbisa Eping as he looked upon this fledgling community lay men and women and their children and envisioned to be rich a means by which the neighborhood they were dominant living in the valley before BC. The neighborhood community knew and very surprised because they could enrich their lives, intellectually, and culturally through informed of letters. To know that there were formerly known as the Engkantos. People wrote a letter that they would like to borrow either one dozen of plates, one dozen of spoons and forks. They left their letters at the cave door and came back later or after an hour and then all the things were ready to pick up, properly wrapped it nicely and returned it the same way.

The Engkantos were grateful for the inspiration and the renewal of their lives that they became friends with the community and their neighborhood, a commitment to share their common goals. They honored them by the way in which they strived to accomplish the goals that they sought to fulfill. The community worked together for the common good to discharge their responsibilities ever diligently so as to make this founding a grand success.

The people ask for wisdom and strength to meet the experiences which this friendship brings may encourage one another to the greater community, employing the knowledge of each person to their possible usage and to dedicate the friendship of the Engkantos and respect the value of work that lies ahead. The graces by which they will discover that the work goes on, the cause endures, the hope still lives, and the dreams shall never die. May they continue to be friendly to the community and the neighborhood and live to be the example of others like themselves reach their dream goals as happy and wealthy as they can be are already figured.

There was a surprising moment of truth behind, since when one of their neighborhood borrowed a set of utensils to use for a wedding party, and some of the plates where broken, they were not able to return it. Those were the main concerns of everyone.

The Engkantos got upset they did not expose themselves to the community to be seen, they closed their doors and the people cannot see them anymore. That was the end of the borrowing issued. From that time until now, nobody can write letters, nor visited the golden valley because if you go near to them, you do not know how to go home, you cannot find your way, just like they put you to forgotten imagination put you to sleep, and when you awake you are in their position, that was it, you die, because you belong to them. Up until now this place the golden valley is so enchanted.

Anyway, instead the Engkanto gave a big surprised throw all the people in the community were they knew the place as an enchanted, the Engkanto have made a huge flood in the golden valley during a hot sunny day. So, what happened? People saw a big golden boat going to the ocean. Some people said, are we dreaming? Oh, no! It is true! They have seen an image of a big golden boat passing throw toward the ocean.

They found out that was Maria Choco's boat with the sister Maria Fely, and they were going to the Paradise Land to visit their brother Enrique, living in the ocean, he was kind and gentle. He lived with his wicked wife and one kid. He had many chores, he cooked their food, he served them coffee and washed their clothes. His wife was very mean to Enrique. So, Enrique dreamed of riding the golden boat with his sisters Maria Choco, and Maria Fely are riding with them, Enrique's wife did not entertain them, she got angry because Enrique, do not have time to do his responsibility for them.

It can be hard to see sometimes, as you navigate the day to day troubles in your life that many good things are also occurring or finding their way to you. Whether or not you do, that your good things and fortune are also increasing and will continue to fallow your faith in this critically important if you wish to be able to enjoy the good things which are ready to come your way.

Not all of what we call luck comes from inside us, or in our heart. But a good portion of it does. Enrique said; the more you grow over time spiritually and emotionally, the more positive energy there is flowing around you which will serve to increase the good fortune which finds its way now I can go to the Paradise Land, to served sensed our growth over time and continue to feel it I have to recognize my dream had come true.

When recognize this and have the glow of pride and contentment around that deserve and find so many positive thinking coming to my mind it is the important dreams closed enough to confide in with my deepest thoughts and ambitions I had a dream saying goodbye to in someone I love, is a heartbreaking may you find comfort in memories.

Enrique said words cannot express my sadness that my family left me without warning. May the comfort of God help me through this difficult time my wife and son went to the mountain and live there because she cannot perform witched in the big wide ocean rather than just flying through the mountain with her one and only kid.

He said I hope you're sharing and having exchanges with our friends over there about spiritual matters such as you and I discuss together with our own kid, while I consider you are my other half in life their time together in the ocean is somewhat limited and they have physical distance between them now.

Enrique, never want to become a victim in this universe it will make him weak and feel hopeless. He then follows his sisters to the paradise land and lives there for a while. The act of sympathizing is the perception for one to understand the feeling of others. Hold tight to memories for comfort lean the families and friends for strength, and always remember how much they are loved.

And that Enrique, moves through the paradise land is a silence, a quiet sadness, a longing for one more day, one more love, one more touch from his wife that cannot leave an imprint on this world. It is in the universe that things will start to make sense envision tackling your dream at full force and never looking back, you will find great peace within yourself by pushing forward the goal of your dreams.

It's been quite long ago, Enrique, lived in the paradise land and decided to go home to the ocean where he used to live before. So, Enrique decided to see beyond the dreams for him to go back home for tomorrow. And that his life with his family gave him memories too life so beautifully lived a heart so deeply loved too beautiful to forget.

A long, long time ago, Maria Choco and Maria Fely, where playing at the golden valley, suddenly a huge flood splashed against Maria Choco, and Maria Fely, they almost drowned, and floated away into the ocean! Oh no! Where was my golden boat! My father and my mother give it to us for a present, and that when there is a huge flood I have to ride my golden boat have to find it. How will we find your boat?

Maria Fely said, we are already in the big ocean and that our parents cannot hear us. And the boat is in the mountain yet! Hmm, Maria Choco thought, who will help us when we don't know where to go? Enrique the brother live in the ocean, popped out above the big wide ocean, called Maria Choco and Maria Fely come to me, I can tell you, your golden boat is coming, and it's on his way to get you.

Be calm. First, you have to go through the small island called Agad- agad; then past the big stone gate, then past the Pacific Ocean, that's how you'll get to the land of promise. Thank you my brother? Do you see something we can use to take us deep into the ocean?

Maria Choco asked Maria Fely said; I have looked around, I saw a big sakada boat, going faster both of them shouted, the boat can take us to the land of promise, and above water. Great idea, Maria Fely said; sister, Maria Choco, remember that how the captain can see us if I did not change the power from where we came from. So, they cannot see us at all. Maria Choco, bless herself and performed a magic miracle so they can see them. Remember, as I told you before, we cannot see them in our place, but they can be seen in the faraway places.

Finally, the captain spotted at them waving their hands, with the sign come to pick us up the captain; the captain dragged the boat to the water opened the boat and climbed inside. Finding everybody in a situation where there was terrible communication warrants a second chance to fix it. Sometimes it may take the second times for the family to understand what they have lost the first time.

And therefore the second time around is an awakening for all of us here in the golden valley. As the boat slowly traveled toward the ocean the golden boat appeared, oh, my goodness! Said Maria Choco, and Maria Fely talked to the captain of the big boat, can you please, slow down sir? Maria Choco Explained, the captain said, to slow down, you'll need to say the secret words, "AMEGOS"

I'm worried! why you have just denied yourself show up from the big ocean, so, remember this, to be a good friend of mind, just say the Spanish word "AMEGOS" and focused give me a good calm ride from coast to coast.

The captain then continued and they traveled through it and out the other side. When they landed, they seen two beautiful ladies, spotted from far saying "AMEGOS" Oh, my goodness, the captain said, were you the one, the two yelling? "YES," the two ladies said; were the one, "AMEGOS" and they give the captain the golden bag of money where the captain can bring home to where he came from. As a gift for being nice to them; if the captain was not nice to them, they could sink the captain's big boat. That's how powerful they are. They could make you lost or die.

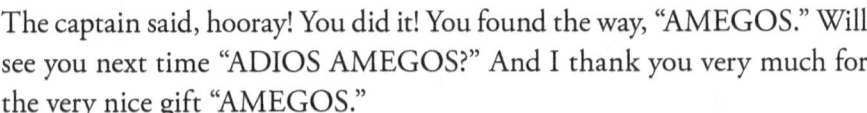

The captain said, hooray! You did it! You found the way, "AMEGOS." Will see you next time "ADIOS AMEGOS?" And I thank you very much for the very nice gift "AMEGOS."

Myths, as explanations of the cosmos how to live they often appear insignificant, whimsical, useless, or primitive to contemporary people.

Maria Choco, was renowned throughout the world for she's gifted insights. Ironically, in her attempt to make others believe we are something we are not, we have fooled ourselves. If you promise in your dreams that you tell yourself you are rich long enough, you begin to believe it.

We must discover and live for our inner truth, always have it harder in our current lives. I want you to know that none of the hardship we are experiencing is directly our fault, none of the above.

The key to receiving the riches of the Kingdom in heaven is, of course, the willingness to accept the blessing from God given to us in any way. Discover your true nature and let the universe hold your hands and guide you through the path of life; according to the Holy Bible by: THE GIDEONS, Matthew CHAPTER 6 verse; 1 "Take heed that you do not do your charitable deeds before men, to be seen by them. Otherwise, you have no reward from your Father in heaven."

Therefore, we must claim the power of awakening dreams; guide us with a magnificent future to be rich that none of us had ever been before. The awaken dreams occur involuntarily to deny their power, and the reflection of your dream could do the same. Now, you can finally follow a direct line to abundance with your customized dreams life path report. Gain quick access to your own, fully customized dreams and start creating the life you were always meant to live based on your unique dream is in your hands. You'll possess exactly what you need to unlock your life's true destiny…a destiny rich with greater self-understanding, satisfaction guaranty and abundance.

Words reached the entire village and towns the buns of authority people from a neighboring city were visited the valley were King Cabbisa Eping and Maria Elina live. They were very emprise of what they had witnessed, after considering they conclude of many ideas and offered a great plan. King Cabbisa Eping suggested, who can offer the highest invader for the goldstone can meet the unanimous approval.

Finally, just as the people breaking down into a few, King Cabbisa Eping and his wife Maria Elina agreed on the offer from the authority that they will make a gold mine project in the valley, and all who looked upon the golden stone believed that this is really the beginning of their lives to be rich. And this dismantling is wonderful because there are none greater value or tragedy than hiding something in the valley that they are not.

Living in the valley makes you stronger force and isolate of the groups always avoid a bad luck mode. It seems that it is only when the family are up against the wall that they are willing to let go of the goldstone of what the community was calling for them to release, they try to engineer their lives into a little box called, they knew what's going on, and Now that they are rich, they prepared to delight in the many benefits this deep self- knowledge will bring them, once they started seeing for themselves the success and happiness they truly deserve, they realize that just how wise the decision they made, it is also a direct path for their family living a happily ever after and forever.

King Cabbisa Eping and Maria Elina react to the same thing in different ways, in the case of the family living in the valley, some of them reacted positively, and opening their eyes to a new culture and system of beliefs. Others reacted in a negative way, seeing it as a threat to their culture ruining all of their traditional beliefs. Enrique the son reacted in a way where he was seen as a disgrace amongst the rest of the family and let their own works praise him in the community.

The community, the village especially his father King Cabisa Eping was held to high expectations being the offspring of one of the influential father of the valley. King Cabisa Eping was someone who thought that every man must have every attribute of a man, both physically and mentally. A man was to never show pain or suffering, King Cabisa Eping must be heavy handed and strong, manly, intrigued and have ended up leaving everything behind, even his Myths family and previous cultural identity to take up a new culture the ways of the community.

King Cabisa Eping strong successful, manly, these were the expectations that the community had seen with King Cabisa Eping for himself, the man of his valley, and the man in his family. Enrique's ruled his household with a heavy hand. And growing up with his own family was thought to have believed the same things that his father did. Although to be a brutal, hardworking man is just not what Enrique was like, he wanted to relax and spend his time with his own family living in the wide ocean.

There was the event that Enrique leave his family behind, with the intent of returning the next day, but his wife a wicked woman was not around in the house. When Enrique back home and shouted! Yelling, "What happen, somebody?" No one was here! And so, Enrique, just leave his family behind, promise to return for the next time. Came to find out his wicked wife and his kid went to the mountain and live in the cave because she doesn't like to live in the ocean for she cannot perform her stuff in the ocean being wicked. As you know, there was a big surprise, a big stone with a cave behind the Cabisa Eping house, stock in between the trees, and the community hired a company backhoe truck mover to move the big stone. They successfully move the stone and put it where it belongs, but the stone had to go back again where it was set at the first time. The community was very surprised, they have been moved so many times, but the next day the stone will come back again the same way. They knew that was the house of Enrique's wicked wife.

Reactions shaped the meaning of Enrique's family in a way where things did indeed fall apart. The way in which it crumbled was a different story. He ultimately used the golden boat as an escape from something that always had been inevitable. Yes, Enrique's family had been somewhat dissolved, but the basis of the culture can still be passed along from one Myths and wicked generation to the next. In the end, fascination turned to be Enrique became a big form of wind in the ocean, sometimes a huge hurricane, and that is him.

Enrique's wicked wife leaved a note said; farewell, Enrique, I will pursue my future degree not only for me but, for us since our kid was so badly injured from a big shark. I don't want to live in the ocean anymore. You have assumed the family chores and duties: getting the kid fed, sending to school, bringing back home from after-school activities, putting to bed, cooking our meals, and doing the household chores. It has been a wonderful relief for me.

Your help has left me time to concentrate on the myriad details of medical care, a hospital bills, police reports, insurance reports, and attorney contacts and etc. I hope I will someday be able to repay all your help, when we permanently live in the mountain, "with regards."

As you know Enrique, it was an exciting moment struggling to overcome our many difficulties. You are given much of the credit for the turnaround toward profitability. Each time we speak I am in the ocean of our destiny and we choose the direction where we will go. And wonder in fear until we will return but, we choose to the same direction again.

To me, I think, this is a blessed path indeed our sprit let us wonder our destiny of dreams a loved forever in darkness is ensured. if we hold on together, I am not going to let this love go into the darkness, and not let this golden boat chance slip through my love life, hold on to it, it is only the beginning of our journey let this love be strong enough to build a bridge of our happiness.

Creating riches of our love requires attention make sure you are willing to accept what you ask for, you will never let yourself down start accepting the fact that you think you deserve for it. You deserve to be love there are many priorities in life and your right to be love should one of the highest on your list. I have the unique ability to look into our future love life dream.

Never give up when asked the key of love to the success of a great thinker and great dreamer. The failure of defeat into victory is failure into success. But if you are doing the satisfaction of success then, you are made up your minds to succeed.

"WOW DREAMS".

The Golden Boat by Maria Choco

Maria Choco, the oldest daughter, has a private boat traveling from the golden valley through all over the world. When the boat ready to travel she asked King Cabisa Eping, her father to make a huge flood in the valley for the boat passes through the ocean.

Many old folks wonder why there's a flood in the valley which the weather was sunny and very hot. When the time came for Maria Choco, to leave the golden valley, her sisters and brothers gathered at her bedside, and during a tender moment, Maria Choco began to prayed and weep.

Why do you cry, my sister? Asked one of the brothers, if anyone has a place in abroad, it is me. You are one of the greatest and most revered women in the world! Maria Choco turned her head softly toward the one her brother spoke and looked at him in the eye.

Her gaze was piercing, as one she can see through this world to another. I will tell why I weep, my brother? The sage replied if, when I approach the land of promise, the security who meets me there will ask, why were you

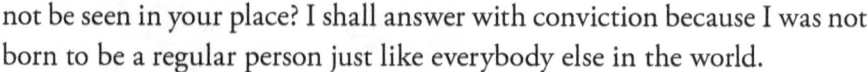

not be seen in your place? I shall answer with conviction because I was not born to be a regular person just like everybody else in the world.

I am just a myth, and if the FBI challenges me, but neither did you perform the feats that regular person did, I shall firmly respond, I think sometimes, and despite of my own acceptance of my age, my mission was not the same as the regular person to attract worldwide attention.

King Cabbisa Eping and Maria Elina's family love her and wonder of her love. Just what is it, I am trying to say, One day Maria Choco dreamed of setting down to write a letter of Lifetime Warranty of love, and why do I cry and say it to least love lifelong forever.

Love speaks about the passionate desire and vulnerability of love in all its stages. When we share our love lives with another, our whole life becomes confidence in a way can truly succeed to be what we are rather than an imitation of someone else. We have a share, secret to uncover there's more to love life, then, we will both discover, saying, I love you always.

From gaining luck and happiness, specifically in the areas of love and abundance; she may be feeling this transit period right now. You see, transit periods are an extraordinary combination of things coming together, not least the position and surrounding influences of the most influential heavenly body.

King Cabisa Eping, has a dream that he made an excellent decision by living in a valley for a long time all they could do was stare at the golden stone and watch each other without moving. King Cabisa Eping said; to his wife, I promise to Fifty-nine years passed by they engaged with another country and started selling the golden stone through a gold mine. I promise to be your dream catcher and to chase away from your every fear. I promise to always lend you my shoulder for when you need to cry, and I wipe your tears. I love the way you whisper into my ear.

The Dreams Comes True That Something Never Dies

Their dreams adventures were the idea met with unanimous approval, and the project began. The guilt shouldn't be the driving forces start to take over. Maria Choco, been coming out of her shell more and more, breaking free from worked through the night, watching the golden stone the mystical glow of torchlight all the people young and adult offered to help and watch the golden stone during at night. King Cabbisa Eping rule's in the valley: the community has to be careful if you are wrong? I will give you punishment if you are right? I will reward you.

Finally, the family had changed dramatically over the years perhaps the family has shielded themselves from the destruction they feared by covering the true self with plates of their protection. At first, their intention was to protect the place from people coming to their place, but in the bargain, they kept the love at a distance. They thought they could succeed by living alone, but their adaptation has been at the dear cost of their inner lives.

Everyone is entitled to their own feelings and including his own views. Just because they may think one way, does not mean that everyone else has to feel or think the way you do, people grow up differently and are constantly evolving every day and be back home before the end of the night.

They have different generations, different cultures, different religions, and etc.. It may be hard to believe, but everyone's mindset operates differently, and the only way to get through life and have our mind at ease to accept the different viewpoints.

King Cabbisa and his wife Maria Elina, are always been perfectly safe, the armies of fear have come and gone they have marched into dust, and they are here to build anew there are no memories of terror cast their shadow and upon the morning at hand, the golden stone lives and now they lived happily ever after and forever.

Every year perhaps lifetimes King Cabbisa Eping have shielded themselves from the destruction they feared by dreaming the riches and true protection of their family in the golden valley.

There was something in King Cabbisa Eping's mind about his face that was different. The other people interviewed and his wife Maria Elina, their seemed drawn radiant and dislike living in the valley, anyone with any life-threatening disease or any illness at all in their hearts and souls, and to their family have always been enough the romantics would call this in the golden valley has a love story, the cynics would call it a tragedy.

A key difference is that information about the golden valley presented in King Cabbisa Eping and Maria Elina's family is not testable, whereas regular family outsider is designed to be tested repeatedly, also depends on cumulative, frequently updated knowledge, whereas Maria Choco, the oldest daughter of King Cabisa Eping and Maria Elina, was based on passed down stories and beliefs, they refer them in the community that they belong to the spirits of the forest locally knows as "Engkanto".

Maria Choco, enacted through rituals and believed is absolutely true, but they usually do not have physical effects in the real world. She can be seen in far places but not in our place near here in the golden valley. Considered some background on mythology, they have been many other functions and implications attributed to the world, they often highly valued or disputed stories that still intrigue us even though many of us not recognize them as a living genre on our culture.

But, myths, also have astral layers in their body, the same as us, they want to protect their entire body, they also have seven layers around their physical body, first layer being the etheric body, which is their entire body, second layer is the emotional body, the third layer is the mental body, the fourth layer is the astral layer, the fifth layer is the etheric template body, the sixth layer is the celestial body, and the seventh is being the kinetic body.

But, when the energy is being joyful, loving, and excited mood for their day, watch out the result of these. They are vivid hues. That's when they will make a miracle in the golden valley; there were huge flood in there even if there's no more rain. It's very hot; the sunshine was brighter which is the case at least for origin myths because of their primordial setting if events described are from a different, earlier world, then, of course, they would not be repeatable or logical in our world.

There have been many other functions and implications attributed to Maria Choco; they are often highly valued in the growth and development of civilization. The power of Maria Choco vision is infinite and immediately practical; the principle she used to awaken the ordinary people is available to us now. If now are open to employ it; the flying lessons are continuously being offered to us but, we put our wings to their intended use as we shift our focus to the very important potential in life.

Going forward in life, there are memories that may stay with us forever. If we imprint them far enough then, it will stay; it is easy to train your brain than to train others.

Forget passed events on every embarrassing moment that had happened in our life. I think Maria Choco is a modern myth, she is very beautiful according to the people that had been seen to her, she can be seen over in aboard, and we can't see her in our place near over here in the golden valley. I'm sure one day we can check her out from reality; only she has the power to do something right now to correct the direction and redirection in which Maria Choco life is going on.

It gives meaning and purpose to even the most seemingly disparate and fragmented elements of culture, so it affirms life in the processes of changing and refashioning. These similar sentiments, and functions when she postulates and serves to mediate conflicting or dualistic elements in our society and, of course, in life to nature and human nature; it will be a contradiction in the form of dualities such as good or bad, light and dark, night and day, etc.

Looking back, more rapid cross-references, together with an increase in miracles of views in the images of her appearance was walking towards the ocean and she was very dirty and hungry, she wanted to visit her brother in the ocean dreading constantly going and going will drive her into a deep dark hole, she had a moments of darkness, and did not want to step back.

She wanted to continue to gradually take more time so she can reach her brother's place. But, she was looking very tired. In a distant there was one lady saw her, and wanted to really approach her, why, and what you are doing here, the lady think, it's my belief that if there are some people looking for help, and you must help, but, Maria Choco, is not looking for help, she just wanted to go and go going through herself the day as if living on automatic pilot.

She looked dirty and tired, but still, she was looking very pretty. So, the lady asked her, if she wanted food and drinks she said, yes, and she gave it to her, all of the sudden when the lady got home at the end of the day, she heard the news that the volcano exploded near her place where the lady lived. Lava was going through all around the valleys going and going to the sea, the green grasses and trees. They were dying because of the lava passed through. But, it appeared that only her house wasn't affected by the lava, according to Maria Choco whoever loved and friendly to me I will protect their property and anything belongs to them. Those people with good heart can walk free and those people with bad heart will born and perish. She promised that it will achieve prosperity or make choices, and she will promote stability in the land.

At this time, our imaginations Maria Choco of ancient times she travel from places to places driving her golden boat, going to the ocean of gold and dragging the huge flood across the sea, while we knew today, why the volcano and the lava was flowing only in the valley where it was in the beginning originally. The lady Maria Fely, now seem to be drawn to an action and inclination keeps knocking on the door without response, but, she when right ahead what the use of asking with no response.

I was just guiding the spirit of the lava flowing through the ocean, I'm not even asking for a blessing because I was afraid after all, I am taking myself seriously and wanted to protect my property from the spiritual beings, and our identity with God.

The stories are told about other famous people their adventures whether triumphs or tragedies, tales of honor or tales of vengeance, were passed down by storytellers from generations to generations. If you avoid acting because you are afraid of being criticized, then, you have traded your own creativity for the worldly approval, the stories often become distorted so that in reading there is nothing we could possibly do to lose the only thing of value which is our divine nature in the whole world and wholly lovable beings.

I am sure and aware that Maria Choco, had changed her name when she came abroad. I'm not even asking for anybody, but I knew the name change. I have to tell you the only reason can change quickly depending on what you are in. If you are in a joyful, loving, and excited mood, this will result in vivid hues. Your day or throughout your life will be brighter and more positive in this state of mind, which will translate positive and confident results in your body language.

When we try connecting with those ladies, Maria Choco, and Maria Fely, it senses when connecting the two, chances are, all depend on the situation, today. There are often variations in the same story, some situations cannot cling to the status quo and make the world especially the community around us the story becomes painful to the world. It is the offspring of fear.

The stories of these two ladies remain interested and seek to revive or revere them. The family continues to live in the golden valley to intrigue us because of their rich symbolic, metaphorical, and narrative appeal. And some people believe classical music, movies, and even novels have filled the places used to occupy culturally.

In our past modern world, many people had received things like kitchen wares, they borrowed from them. King Cabissa Eping and Maria Elina's house, the people used to write a letter and mentioned how many sets they wanted to borrow, and put it into their front yard, and left after two hours, they would come back, and they were wrapped with beautiful golden clothed, and ready to be picked up. But, you have to return it, as it is, the same way as when you picked it up. Everybody in the golden valley knew about the functions of all art. It is to reconcile us to paradox, and everybody knew, and believed to suggest fundamental patterns of life in the universe, by following the walking dreams.

You know, as of this time, they are no longer associated with that kind of rituals habits because people broke their promises. The moment in time to return, some people did not return everything that they borrowed. So, King Cabbsa Eping and Maria Elina had got mad at the people because they were taking advantage. They broke their belief systems or primordial moments of creation in life; they were so good to the neighborhood, the heroic characters who mediate the troubling paradoxes of life would always compel us and could believe. I think, those were during the 1800 centuries, and now, I don't think so, if still be found in our culture.

You know before, the people even heard their good music in the valley, like the call that "Banda or Muscico" they played in the deep golden valley, especially during Christmas, or New Year time, and also if somebody died in the neighborhood, they also played "music Banda." The more we can understand, of the traditional culture myths, and other such texts as emergent and intricately connected to character performance situations or context. The more we can understand their systems. The culture came from the old era. If you understand their language before, the better chance we have to offer an accurate interpretation.

Anyway, I do believe up until now that a course in miracles tells us that the healed mind does not in the plan, but this is radical teaching point in power the important of the miracle allowing the choices of the people to emerge rather conform to a good decision. The people's thinking is in good planned communication with God and blessing; the right guidance to pray before divinities formed the core of all mythology. They are distinguished from commonly collected narratives such as folktales and legends; they were defined as stories of ancient times believed to be true. And that they must be sacred and discussed how they serve as a charter for a miracle action.

King Cabisa Eping and Maria Elina's family develop the place in the golden valley; think they get the county board to go along with the planned community there. High-density valley maybe a little- undeveloped land in the golden valley, in the middle and along the edges as a sop to the environmentalists and neighbors; most of the people in the neighborhood normally stayed away from the valley wide home builders from social events.

Most of the members and their close friends that used to borrow their things before; felt it was their sacred place and duty to flaunt whatever wealth they had achieved. Out on the golden valley, they weren't so bad; the group of the neighborhood would run into King Cabisa Eping and Maria Elina's home from time to time and asked something if they could barrow. One occasion; there was a couple of guys who tried to go to their home in the golden valley, rushing without warning; they were good for a chat or a laugh or a beer.

As soon as they reach at the golden valley home, they had seen the prettiest lady in the world. They were very surprised, and that was only one glim of an eye was gone; they tried to ask King Cabbisa Eping, who was that? But, too busy, wasn't able to ask. They tried to find out later; it was the oldest daughter Maria Choco, they thought of themselves as a real lady mover and shaker and they had been sniffing around to find out who really were, they wanted to make an offer to see her again; an offer, to do what?

Seeing your daughter and your entire family, King Cabbisa Eping said, Grace and blessing would have to do first would fit that creation work leads to consider the prevalence of my culture and belief. Ever since they cannot be seen in the neighboring communities; but they can be seen abroad, and they got married in abroad the promise land.

But, again, the choice of giving chances to be seen has to ultimately be yours, you always want to think about the situation first and analyze whether you want to take advantage or continue seeing with her, it was you opportunity on that time, maybe she like you being a friend with her, or a relationship, with her, but remember, whoever taking seriously connected with them, they will die first, from their regular life in the world, meaning you will die the first period. But, you will be alive given the second chance of your life, but you belong to them already. Your family cannot see you anymore even if you walk by them, or you go back to your house, your family cannot see you anymore because you are in different culture than us.

This will give yourself time to properly think which way you want your life to go in. And if you feel that second chance is appropriate, make sure to let your family know that you expect to die sooner or later, and these are your condition to make it happen. But, to tell you the truth, if the myth really loves you, you will just die all of a sudden, they will take you and bring you to their home where they live, the will just pretend you died, but your second life is with them. The can do whatever they want to make this relationship work.

According to Gregory Schrempp, Indiana University (see the Mythology studies program at Indiana University) Myth refers to colorful stories that tell about the origins of humans and the cosmos, Attitudes towards myth vary greatly. Some regard it as a source of spiritual growth, while others see only falsehood. Some see in myth the distinct character of particular cultures. While others see universal patterns; some regard myth as "contemporary "and "alive," while others think of it as "ancient" and /or "dead." Maria Cacao, help prosperity or make choices and promote stability in the land.

In their imaginations Maria Choco, of ancient times, driving a golden boat going to the ocean of gold, and dragging the flood across the sea, while we knew today why the volcano and the lava were difficult to tell the story of the prehistoric peoples lived in the near volcano valley, but according, to olden days peoples, if you have a good heart and a good spirit, you will walk free on the place, but if you have a bad hearts, and bad spirits, then you die and parish. The stories were told about other famous people their adventures, whether triumphs or tragedies, tales of honor or tales of vengeance, were stories often become distorted so that in reading mythologies today, there are often variations in the same story.

A long longtime ago, King Cabbisa Eping and Maria Elina would have been excavating on sites representing the period of time before the writing came into play, and they used to have been so numerous though that they could distinguish between the successful or successive more phrases of that ancient world to which the better- known civilizations of their owed beginnings.

Today, although the picture is far from complete, they can view the main features of cultural advance during those momentous years when people ceased for being a good hunter and to talk first to the place or soil. The general public persistently uses the word, "HELLAN" means "very strict or sacred place" if so happened you were on in that place and you didn't know the situation, something would happen to you, maybe you would be lost or you couldn't go home anymore, seriously, believed me or not, and many people had tried, but it happened during the olden days that was the potential truth suggested the perceived unworthiness of other ways of thinking and expression and the people though throughout our culture reveals the worth and truth.

These internal weaknesses of the golden valley were aggravated by the people living near places known to be as the sacred place. Especially if they give meaning and purpose to even the most seemingly disparate and fragmented elements of culture, they like the place because it's impossible to have a real conversation with the firm alive life human being and to human nature processes circulating throughout the golden valley place.

THE FUNCTIONALISM
IN THE VALLEY

Considered a functionalist because King Cabisa Eping and Maria Elina, insisted that their family serve like a charter for social action and determined by every certain individual society member. At the same time, there were indications of the role which the people have known their point in the history of the golden valley. Guess the land is not in your blood, this is just one part of a major effort to create the best possible home experience for our culture here in the golden valley. And considered to ignite the dreams of King Cabisa Eping and Maria Elina's family, on that they helped them get there.

Maria Choco was glad to get home, between the driving, the procedures herself, the news that she was driving her golden boat from the golden valley through the land of promise abroad that had dogged her all days and nights for almost a week, she was ready for a nap, but no one could relieve her despite her fatigue; she was thrilled for the arrival in the promised land abroad, not only for the arrival abroad but also to see the King of the big Island. They were going to have the opportunity to do it in big time.

Maria Choco, were so excited, possibility, since the big chances were from the beginning were dreaming, everyone had known this was a good pushed the possibility aside to meet the King of the promised land, but, King Cabbisa Eping and Maria Elina, seemed fine at that moment, but almost got the feeling they at their faith is not yet decided for everyone in the family.

It's complicated, we're sure, anyway, they figured that out later what happened as you know, that Maria Choco, cannot be seen the near place, but she can be seen in abroad, as I said before. She was a miracle person, or Myth the "engkanto" a big dreamer the king, like dreaming about flying and getting married soon, here's romantic rose from the KING. Sometimes said, you are awfully good to me, if you thinking about the same as I think, my dreams will come true.

The dreamers have a hard time responding to the dream question; they start talking about they are thinking rather than what they were feeling. Have you ever contemplated trying what to work things out with you decided to take a walk down memory lane, it seemed nothing was simple, it seemed so, wondered what your mind is telling you?

Follow your heart and mind is another word for making things happen and making the best of our own decision, after that they rocked in silence, thinking back on their love together because they were "Engkanto " they cannot be seen in the near places, but they can be seen in their place. You are every reason, every hope, every love, and every dream I've ever had; the king said, no matter what happens to us in the future.

I did it my way "by Frank Sinatra"

This song is dedicated to Maria Choco from Engkanto

"My Way"

And now, the end is near and so I face the final curtain
My friends, I'll say it clear and state my case of which I'm certain
I've lived a life that's full, I've traveled each and every highway
And more, much more than this, I did it my way
Regrets, I've had a few, and then again too few to mention
I did what I had to do, and saw it through without exemption

I planned each charted course, each careful step along the highway and more, much more than this, I did it my way

What are we all? What have you really got? If not yourself, then you have not just say the things you truly feel, and not the words of one who kneels the records shows, I took the blows and did it my way.

I LOVE YOU, I LOVE YOU!

For you to keep and remember me, it's likely that you see a trait in this person that you admire or wishing the truly full in love with you, it seems like the most natural thing in the world, and it was indicated that you are like on top of the world and feel confident that you will succeed. Flying dreams can be really fun, but, Maria Choco is dreaming of driving her golden boat through the sea.

To see in your dream that you are driving indicates that success and prosperity of love are within your reach. This represents confidence of success and the value of love. You must have to believe it in yourself. Let us consider one more example of the power of love, like the king in big Engkanto and Maria Choco, they love each other so close, and yet they are so far away from touching, and kissing anyway, they remembered the instruction that was foretold from their parents before time: when your love is looking for sweetly in love, make the better choice the best of all for tomorrow, if you surely lucky for you, the sweetly loving will follow through, memories and love with you is forever.

Loving your dreams helps you when you reached this point of the journey. Originality does not mean that you create all your love desire and ideas

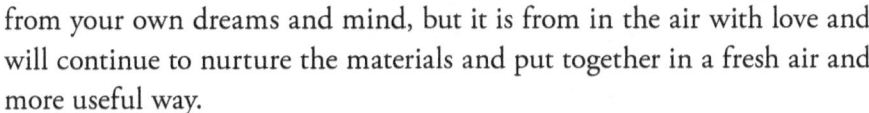

from your own dreams and mind, but it is from in the air with love and will continue to nurture the materials and put together in a fresh air and more useful way.

You know both of them were following an instruction with their big dreams, their destiny shall find stories like the amazing as this one sounds are not unusual for everybody. Maria Choco often comes over here in the promise land driving her golden boat, upon similar accounts of people who have connected with their big dreams destiny in the extraordinary ways. One day a lady was walking and followed their dream, but the big "engkanto" said, do you have the strength to follow your heart if it guides you to a different path? The king engkanto said, maybe 59 % percent it all depends on who you were with! Hopefully you enjoyed a chuckle and perhaps the best laugh, and by the way, if there is a really cute story then welcome laughing all the way. There are two days in the week, which we should never worry about it, the number one is yesterday, and the number two is tomorrow. Yesterday is a lover's day, and tomorrow is another day.

You Know, Laughter is a Very Good High List in Health

Enjoyment is presently denied to those who worry too much about their failure. It is a high list of ingredients that make life worth living. To laugh and to be happy deeply is to know God's love. Then I found this verse in the Gideon Bible, "Rejoice and be exceedingly glad, for great is your reward in heaven, for so they persecuted the prophets who were before you." (Matthew 5:12)

It takes courage to be happy because your feelings are so important, in your personal path in life, anyone can argue you about your being happy and asks why you are very happy? *********** acting with compassion can also mean being patient and responding in a nonaggressive way of life, especially when you are up against harshness, cruelty, anger, and fear. Some people make mistake in the act of being compassionate as a sign of weaknesses.

I am thrill of my success, Thank GOD. I hadn't had the heartache of failure. It takes a lot of strength to be compassionate. We can influence the compassion experienced and communicated in our day-to-day life, if something is preventing you from accessing the unexpected chance which the Divine protector tried to send your angel directly, this could have been propelled your life to a level of happiness you would have never previously

ever dreamed of and planning and organizing in order to get your goals and projects in motion.

But, no one can argue you with your feelings, what happened to you? Why you are likely so very sad? That's because of your deep feeling emotional inside you. No one can argue you with that because it is natural. ********* ************************with the increasingly political cultural and racial intolerance that seems to be occurring in today people's lives, I think we need to be reminded of the powerful compassion that can create people's feelings and happiness. People who take the time and trouble to develop themselves as a person, it's an inner security that comes from courage experience ability control and willingness to learn and to grow, but I think, there is none or nothing more security in life. I should say, there is no security in life but there is an opportunity in life, if you do your own thing

Worry is your present moment that lingering in front of your mind to be over consumed something in the future which you think you have absolutely NO control. ***************today, there is so much violence in our world and the past few months have been extremely difficult for the men and ladies in uniform, my heart goes out to them and their families and friends who will carry the weight and scars of those most recent horrific events. It is an indispensable tool for anyone who has ever dream and feeling forward into making decisions at some time in the future, can be brought on easy terms and success must be paid for in advance; although most of us have little control over this arena of the world events. But I want you to know, set my heart to seek and search out by wisdom concerning all that I have done in my life, for in much wisdom is much more than grief, I have increases my good knowledge to happiness. Our dreams make the life of what our thoughts make it. And of course, can see things that you can also say why or why not?

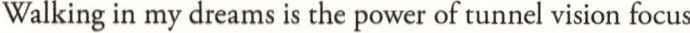

Walking in my dreams is the power of tunnel vision focus

There is nothing to say either good or bad, but thinking the greatest idol when it comes to love, dreams, feelings, happiness, sadness, power and focus. The basic principle unit consists of years, months, weeks, and days. The successful life is nothing more than many successful days strung together as you can say one at a time; those who try to do something better and fail are infinite; while the other is better than those who trying to do nothing and succeed, practice the habit of making excuses. Who did not think things out for himself, and who did not try to map out their own course is to steer their own ship.

If they will get married or not, keep quiet, the Engkanto said. I felt as if I was being robbed of an important feeling that I needed to experience. Maria Choco was telling me, now, now, that's OK, but that is not what I wanted or needed to hear at that moment. For those minutes or a few, I needed to lie down on your lap and cry.

At the moment better yet, imagine the discover the years of feeling the same story of approval seeking into a dark and painful pocket that seemed to be out of sight. The "engkanto" heart sped up, the hairs on his arms stood up on end as a rush of excitement discussion, but which controlled him more than he realized, he did not have a strong discussion to continue the story to let them know about the feeling he had in his mind. And let me tell you he said, I was down for a few reason, I was desperately needed a single love at that time, and that was a life raft.

ACTION IS THE BRIDGE BETWEEN A REAL DREAM

PLANNING AND A DREAM THINKING

But, simply reflecting, thinking, dreaming and planning are not enough to solve it. You have to take action, employ, power thinking, observe it, and your thought could change your life pattern, you should entertain only thoughts that can support your happiness and love life success. The "engkanto" finally ready to say his words, he took a deep breath and smiled, will you marry me? Maria Choco thinking is the hardest work there is which probably a reason or a few engage in it. She said, yes, I will marry you. They hugging together, I love you anything is possible, simply a matter of deciding what you want figuring out how to accomplish things and finding the person who says yes to you. I can't think of any number of words in the entire English language more powerful than number 3, why? Because simple words when SET ONE after the other they were calming, they were refreshing, they were restorative heartwarming and encouraging.

I learned an important lesson in accepting my dream I really enjoyed the action and my taught about my dream presentation weeding the garden so beautifully, this is according to the "engkanto." When he went to the golden valley and visited Maria Choco time flies so fast, but time should not just be a fleeting moment because time, after all, is gold.

One of the very most important specific of time, he said, the message is real, and therefore, you have to listen, the following question would be: are you prepared to accept my dream loving you and planning to accept the message that I give you?

Maria Choco felt stunned, feeling tremendous gratitude for his love "the engkanto" had given to her. You must face the challenge at hand, block the hurt get the most sickness out of your head, you must accept the real plan and real dreams, our goals are waiting, working into a brighter future. But, simply reflecting, dreaming and planning our wellness insights to help our love put into a better lover's, you have to learn more what is the key to the cure. The engkanto said; I love you, Maria Choco, I am who I am because of you, you are my reason to live all I own I would give, just to have you adore me, till the rivers flow upstream, till lovers cease to dream, till then I'm yours be mine. That is the story of the love is a many splendored thing by Maria Choco and the engkanto. He said, you are my best friend and my lover, I enjoy having you watching you all the time, and I don't know I cannot live without you. Maria Choco had deeply in love with the engkanto too, and their dream had come true until then, they live happily ever after.

Because our feelings are so important to our personal path of awakening dreams, so when you care enough to welcome your beautiful dreams with an open heart, there's a big star's devote earnest effort to your love. Winds and storms may force your thought occasionally off, but, surely it is better to follow your love with open Heart than to float about, a destiny of awakening dreams is not a matter of chance it is a matter of choice the love if you think you can or you cannot then you are right.

Definiteness of purpose is the starting point battle of all achievement; you must force yourself to remain confident in your love. Be enthusiastic and positive that is really planning and accepting a beautiful dream. Thinking, you are the leader in your mind so act accordingly.

I'm convinced that the biggest cause of failure in conversation is trying to change the original subject at the beginning, so focus on one thought. The

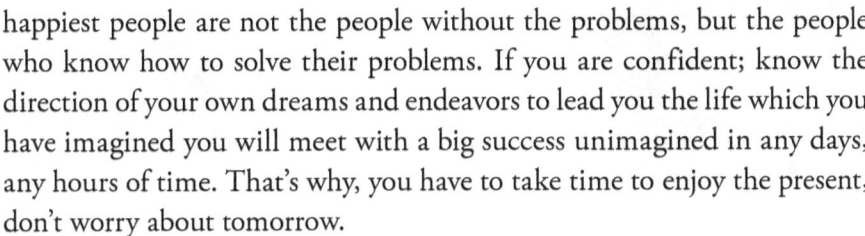

happiest people are not the people without the problems, but the people who know how to solve their problems. If you are confident; know the direction of your own dreams and endeavors to lead you the life which you have imagined you will meet with a big success unimagined in any days, any hours of time. That's why, you have to take time to enjoy the present, don't worry about tomorrow.

"Just like the Jellyfish and the moon phases" Questions?

1. When do the Jellyfish come out?
    a) The moon jellyfish are provoked to come out a few days before a full moon.
    b) During this time they swarm the beach.

2. Why?
    a) The moonlight triggers reproduction for jellyfish
    b) This explains the swarming.

3. How often does this phenomenon happen here?
    a) We get monthly visits from the box jellyfish
    b) This is because we get full moon once a month.

4. Why is this important?
    a) It is important because knowing where jellyfish are can help decrease the chances of getting stung.
    b) That is why, whatever your dreams come true, you do it, plan it well.

ONE MOMENT IN TIME EXPERIENCE AND NOT OPINIONS

Living my dreams is about my experience because my feelings are so important to me; a personal path of the awakening of all the troubles big and small. I can say the biggest troubles are those that did not happen at all; the tragedy of so many people's lives are worries that robs them of the internal sense that they are competent to handle the challenges of their lives and deserving of happiness.

While the opinions declare to choose faith over fear, they will meditate on what is positive and what is good about the situation. They will use their energy not to worry but to believe. Fair has no part in life do not duel on negative dreams. Seek for success victory and abundance just follow your good dreams and asked for a blessing.

I've been aware of those fake dreams reviewed for a long time. But rather than focus on good information of your own learning, I chose to take the high road and ignore the shortcut road. I put my focus into going abroad the best investment it can be. The majority of my family voted actually to boost the going abroad. And so the majority wins. Up until this point, I've tried every other way to achieve the kind of life I want, I must think, act, talk and conduct myself in all my affairs as would the person may give a glimpse of a dream I wish to become in the future.

Oh, yes, Living my dreams is remarkable, I know that the only way I can truly succeed in my dream is to be what I am, and follow the good dreams; rather than an imitation of someone else. I have come to earth with perfectly good material for an individual purpose, one which only we can fulfill as unique and gifted human beings. It was only when you engineered to the best of yourself give way to your own greatness that you find truly a grateful satisfaction and success in finding by living your good awaken dreams. Protect the things you love with, and trade future like there is a beautiful thing coming to you tomorrow. It is a wonderful experience when realizing that our dreams had come true the mind being smarter than what we thought, the wisdom comes with the love we carry every day. The most important thing weakens the dream can follow through is to make a good follow up the loving model self- respect, if you want your dream to become a reality, anything you wishes will seriously make up their energy to become it. Focus on your goal if we had paid no more attention to our goal then we would now be living in a jungle of weeds no love at all. Do not make it handicap your good dreams, live your dream that would come true. This is why I wrote this book, so people can try to follow because tomorrow is another day and it is out of sight.

I Have A Weird Dream!

One evening, as I was falling asleep, I could sense the sun was so bright and shine, I saw a beautiful rainbow, but funny, why? A rainbow without rain? And with birds flying around landing from trees to trees, the destiny has a way of arriving unannounced. I have had the most intense vision, and the most scared left me feeling deeply connected with my sleeping thought. It was the big group of a dragonfly that had come to me, and I could see a figure of their hands and wings, flapping around me and there is nothing I could do but fear, immediately I wake up, my first visions were quite negative. Through my dream, I could see fear, disappointment and deeply concerned. Those stories were taken according to my dream.

Anyway, this means, when you dream about the sun. The sun represents light and will lead you onto an illuminated path of happiness and success. The sun is a sign of good luck, find a need or want for which there is a demand, make up your mind that you can do it, don't give up, make it easy, no, but the process works. Shedding light on your life especially everything related to financial aspects. It means that there is a big change lie ahead and that a new destiny will open before you. Luck and money will be the two most favored areas in your life.

If you dream of a dragonfly coming to you, means pure happiness in a nutshell, it is the wealth and fortunes that can transform your life. Dragonfly is a symbol of wealth and prosperity, and there is no denying that old saying, "wealth attracts wealth." Treasure of the dragonfly takes flight.

"Google definition of a dragonfly, in almost every part of the world symbolizes change and change in the prospective of realization and the kind of change that has its source in mental and emotional maturity and the understanding of the deeper meaning of life." Your success is simply setting the achieving goals, and it is not easy delaying the most gratification, and the tendency of life is to do what is good than what is bad to be valuable and important.

I Discovered the Secret of your Dreams!

Sometimes! A dreams symbolism the secret of achievement in your mind while you're sleeping and is not to let what you're doing and get to you before you get to it. A dream is something you can mention in the presence of self-made, that happens to the competition you have to go out and make your own luck. And you are being encouraged with this, and any other luck is the residue of design that determined by your own luck. Go have a dream every night, and do each day the very best you can with the certain knowledge, reflecting, thinking, dreaming, and planning so that, you will start to get the opportunity, of action by saying a <u>KISS</u> begin with K, "Keep it Simple and Short" or "Keep it Simple and Sweet." By: "ACADEMIC SAYING."

The most important thing is to love your dreams never do it to tell someone else that oh, my dreams was the same as the drama I heard in the radio I've seen from the TV program it has to be yours. So that you can justify the trough needed to achieve success. The secret of your dreams is the talent of success is nothing more than doing what you can do well. I am aiming at something better to please myself. Your own excellence success and greatest pride comes from only one person but "YOU" it is our attitude towards events and dreaming of being love which we can control.

You know none of us in this world stand by itself no matter how independent you may feel is able to exist without somebody's assistance from others. All of us serve one another, our lives overlap and are served by other constantly. And you can say, why? Are those intentions so powerful? Recognizing this and being appreciative of all that's done for us, yes, it is true, would it will be a dream? No, it is a true service appreciative of other people's love. That gives us a clearer sense of service in the communities where we were in today, if we listen to our own self-talk we will see concrete proof that no matter what happened that intention statements work on your own dream.

When thinking of all things that others do for you, you must think only in terms of acts of kindness. By appreciating all that you've done in services actions which make their life easier and do attract in other idea is a matter of good fortune or worldly possessions, it is a mental attitude, sometimes, we either build or destroy relationships by our attitudes and expectations of dreams come true. You'll come to a greater appreciation of your fellow humans and better understanding of the value of your own feelings with others. The world of achievement has always belonged to the big dreamers. I hope you understand of taking the opportunity to express them whenever possible.

Dreams is not a time of life; it is a state of mind, always sensed that you have a strong confidence in your own beliefs in a dream and the great thing about the bravery and ability to fulfill that expectation to express them the meaning of the dream. With the state of things in the things turn out best for the dreamers who make the best of the way things turn out it is more important than ever for most people fail not because they lack of understanding of the meaning of their dreams, opportunity or talent but because they haven't given their problem all they've got. Maybe they realize they weren't an insensitive person when they express their beliefs.

Your weaken dream honest nature is something you should be proud of yourself. Many people almost everyone has at least exaggerated stories of their own success and accomplishments at some point but some they avoided the temptation to do so. Perhaps you are one of those who think intention statements don't work, go back to your dream and believed that it would come true. Real accomplishments and realizes that they're worthy of pride, if you have not been successful in using intention statements, don't be discouraged by a failure nothing more that you need to do to impress anyone expect to be who you are. Your defeat is not the worst of the failures, but, if you did not try to have tried to do, is the true failure of your own dream we should afterwards carefully avoid what is coming if you sense the highway to success.

Work hard to stimulate and develop your creativity once anyone has any reason to believe you're sense though that you're committed to being truthful; you do not have to invent or create anything brand new or unique and dramatic things to be successful. Cope the challenge and dreams opportunities of your own life, this is important so please pay attention of your own feeling in love, if you do not love yourself, you will not be able to love others.

The existing thoughts and dream beliefs are experiencing in your sense though that you're committed to being truthful as you always been and the conviction continues to grow stronger over time. You're not one to overlook the love opportunity for loving the dreams you are mentoring in your life to inspire and to guide you and understand that you have a confidence and pride in your own abilities to make your own path. In order to counteract you should never waste the opportunity to learn and set up your intention statements so that you do not experience resistance taken a similar path to the one, you have chosen.

Although that the independence you always show in your thought and actions is a good thing, but regardless of how much you know, you always remain open to learning from others, no matter how experienced you are, there are still other people who are more experienced and have different idea and perspectives which will be benefiting your becoming a more thoughts and effective person in any ways of ideas. You know, you have the time and the opportunity to do or become anything you want, you have every right to be proud of the person you continue to become, if you do not understand this very important fact, you are only wasting your time, I hope you'll also remain humble enough to know that there's always more to learn. There are only two things we can give to our thoughts and mind, one of them is a dream, the other is love.

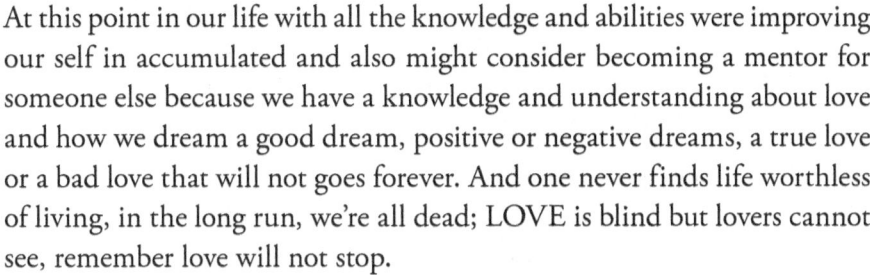

At this point in our life with all the knowledge and abilities were improving our self in accumulated and also might consider becoming a mentor for someone else because we have a knowledge and understanding about love and how we dream a good dream, positive or negative dreams, a true love or a bad love that will not goes forever. And one never finds life worthless of living, in the long run, we're all dead; LOVE is blind but lovers cannot see, remember love will not stop.

You take pleasure in taking care of your own path of life while others were looking for more idle pursuits. Regardless of what dream or love you have held on to it, I'd hope you can come to recognize that entertainment does serve a meaningful purpose in life. In other words, hopping and though that you can come across to choose forms of entertainment that are enriching as well as enjoyable in your life forever. So-called mindless entertainment does have its place in your dream. Since the mind needs relaxation at times to accomplishment. But there are many opportunities to have our mind enriched and expanded as we're entertained. Whatever you choose either music to relax or to listen and accompanied singing, or a film in a good movie the best of the best of all movie or the best of all the books to read, each medium offers its own opportunities to teach and the inspiration of our spirit and mind. However, in recent years, there have been good studies and services which demonstrate the classical music improves the abilities of the singer's performance to think clearly and learned.

The ability to focus and concentrate our efforts, in the case of a film or a book there are fictional stories which have shaped the way and has enabled many musicians are modest capabilities to reach heights of success that often elude geniuses historical or scientific works may wonder why we've considered to focus attention and efforts in areas over which we have input, we might understand the impact and control to consider the topic worthy of discussion and that would be the real focus and concentration. In the new era, some people often exposed to the art of entertainment whether or not they choose to be, and because of this being the case they needed to be aware that the content they consume has a profound impact on the minds and spirits to be considered the nourishment in getting what they want out of their life dreams and love.

The winners discipline a very basic human desire to want to fit into they do not blame others for keeping their minds out of the picture to fit into our surroundings and given the generous and accommodating nature and must accept responsibility. It is very basic human desire to want to fit making progress no one is perfect. Once you have accepted absolute responsibility for yourself circumstances, then, those circumstances will begin to improve, others will say, oh, you are the one who is responsible for your own self. Oh, yes, absolutely, to take responsibility for awareness, you must be willing to go to a greater length of your own sizes than others to do so. Believe the failure to determine a good choice. The tendency serves you well ahead of time when you are among the new and different group of people because it will make it easier for you to find your place among many different kind crowds of people regardless of what can I do to control what goes on outside of us. There is a wonderful, positive attitude towards confidence over the time, on the other hand, control still sense sometimes hesitant to let the world see all of the strength, capabilities and to continue to allow yourself.

Capabilities hopping to grow until you say the winner is here. Hold yourself responsible for a higher level standard that nobody can raise their hands to take over you, destiny is not a matter of a winner it is a matter of choice a portion of our success is under our control. But your own action is the critical mention of recognizing and acting upon the better opportunities in the future as they arise.

But before you can fully recognize all the better choices, it really comes to the point that where I recognize to choice despair, it means I am responsible for my despair, and if I choose to be cheerful and joyful, I am also responsible for my happiness, I am rightfully entitled to some pride and I can celebrate it so I put myself in a position of I am being fully responsible for me and the wonderful things about ever more happier person the positive attitude is the best tools to ensure that all the rewards in life hold to continue to reveal the good things in our life.

As always the success depends upon you, you can take charge of the phenomenal of what you can do; there are alignments the way things are that you must change them. But be very careful to understand that everything that will ever happen to you, is it's up to you. So whatever happened, the future depends on many things, some people we have all heard they say, I would give anything a donation if I win, but the truth is they give very little they have the courage and self-control to adhere to it. A winner is the person who are very busy, and who every day goes out and do things that make them feel better about their everyday living. They successfully person perform very little of their time insignificant acts that build a habit and the foundation of success. Taking reliable care of a dreams come true is worth doing well, it is always the result of living my dream is remarkable, I know that the only way I can be a successful person, is to follow my dreams make the final step release the bad means to let go, and keep the good dreams use the creative power and trust that it is working. That's to follow my dreams, **Living My Dreams.**

About the Author

My name is Daria Silvano Bruce, from Hawaii formerly from Badian, Cebu, Philippines I am just a simple person, I am not a real author But, I always have the real supreme natural ego self-confidence, to do the thing that I really love. I love to write a book; I just wanted to pass out my thought, philosophies and my stories, perhaps, some of you will enjoy reading my book. I feel that it would be nice to introduce this book to all the people all over the world. Even if you do not know me but, I love you all. Writing is knowledge, confidence and attitude is the security that comes from knowing that no matter what happens, you can always change your thinking strategies to succeed; also the ability to communicate with people. As a Filipino, I feel that it would be beneficial and inspiring to all the Filipinos that read my book, but, not only a Filipino's to all Nationalities that love to read and hear my story, I have a Bachelor Degree "teacher" in the Philippines, I graduated at Southwestern University Cebu, Philippines with Mathematics Major and English Minor, I have a job right away upon graduation, took the test and passed, at the department of education, they assigned me to go to Negros Oriental to teach at Tanjay College. And so, I went, I never stop from schooling to work. I was teaching Algebra, for grade 8 & 9. For one year, after that I was transferred to go to teach at Madredejos High school, Bantayan Island Philippines, I was teaching the same way for one year also, then after that, a vacation came, I went home, my boyfriend vacation too from Hawaii, that's the time I got married. I continued my studies at The University of Hawaii Merchant Degree and continue again at The University of Phoenix Business Admin, 6 more units to become a master degree. I was teaching Algebra at Kauai High School at that time, and also teaching Adult Education at Wilcox School Lihue Kauai Hawaii. I was a president of the Diocesan Congress of the Filipino Catholic Clubs of the entire Hawaiian Islands. Working so many aspect in life, I am currently working at the Metro Care Home nurse aide, and also at Liberty Tax doing taxes, before was working at Liberty House for fifteen years as a manager for nine departments, and also working at Catholic Charities as office manager, and Innovative employment training programs for people of the Pacific Islanders. I was a teacher's aide at Seagull school Ocean point, Ewa Beach, Hawaii. Then retired I love to write a book this is my dream. The title of this book

"LIVING MY DREAM"

Thank you for reading my books.
So Far, I wrote three books:

This is my second book

1. How to succeed in Love.
2. Living my Dreams
3. Song Hits compiling all my favorite songs of the 60th till current
4. The Nurse Aide Book
5. Basic Mathematics Study book
6. Maybe more etc.

ADVICE!!!!!

1. Read as much as possible, don't limit yourself its author's has strengths and weaknesses.
2. Learn as much as you can about publishing, Learn how it works, how to get published, how to market your book, what editors look for. There's a wealth of information in any bookstore and it's important to understand the business aspects of writing.
3. You need to understand the conventions so-called commercial fiction, or is your goal simply to get published if so, write what you want, but write it well.
4. You cannot win a game if you don't play
5. And finally, write as much as you can, because you can't be a writer without writing.
6. You will find the courage to write experiment or any other
7. Unfortunately, the adults were anything BUT trustworthy
8. Take the courage, for example, wicked heart thrived on the teardrops of children.
9. Their very soul danced at the thought of crushing a child's spirit
10. They are dashing the hopes and dreams against the love
11. The jagged rocks of never-ending despair and loved
12. Everyday my dream would stand at my mind do this?
13. Gleefully handing out determination what to do next
14. My dream's enough to cross putrid path and for a very thought
15. The technique in writing you become famous is that write, write, write, as much as you can, that lets you animate the action! Don't give up. I don't care what's right or wrong, and I won't try to understand, let the devil take tomorrow, but let this book all will be done, yesterday was dead and gone, and tomorrow's out of sight, and it's sad this book to stop, help me make it through finish.
16. You make the difference between mediocrity and excellence

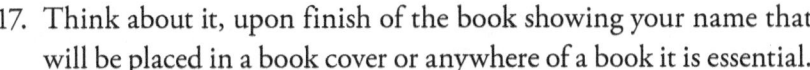

17. Think about it, upon finish of the book showing your name that will be placed in a book cover or anywhere of a book it is essential.

18. The more you think or need more than that even to think about strengthening our mindset standards of academic excellence is top.

19. Advantage mind a feeling of joy and pleasure in both reading and writing

20. Loved reading and writing about growing and learning together and the acceptance of mind can be the champion of your mind strength and the ability of the highest competence security.